ROYAL AMBASSADORS

BRITISH ROYALTIES IN
SOUTHERN AFRICA 1860–1947

THEO ARONSON

THISTLE
PUBLISHING

This edition published in 2014 by:

Thistle Publishing
36 Great Smith Street
London
SW1P 3BU

www.thistlepublishing.co.uk

ISBN-13: 978-1-909869-99-8

ROYAL AMBASSADORS

Victoria
1819-1901
m.
Albert
1819-1861

1 other *Edward VII* *1 other*   *ALFRED* *HELENA* *4 others*
1841-1910   *1844-1900* *1846-1923*
m.   *m.*
Alexandra   *Christian*
1844-1925   *1831-1917*

ALBERT *GEORGE V* *3 others*   *Christian* *VICTORIA* *3 others*
VICTOR *1865-1936*   *Victor* *1870-1948*
(Eddy)   *m.*   *1867-1900*
1864-1892 *MARY*
1867-1953

EDWARD VIII   *GEORGE VI*   *4 others*
1894-1972   *1895-1952*
m.   *m.*
Wallis   *ELIZABETH*
Simpson   *b. 1900*
b. 1896

ELIZABETH II   *MARGARET*
b. 1926   *b. 1930*

For Brocas Harris

Contents

Preface	xi
Prince Alfred	1
Prince Eddy And Prince George	45
Prince George And Princess May	71
Princess Christian	95
The Prince Of Wales	115
The Royal Family	155
Epilogue	216
Bibliography	220
Notes	225

Grateful acknowledgements are due to the following for illustrations reproduced on the pages specified: Burke's Peerage (Royal Arms, page 6); South African Library (10, 17, 25, 32–3, 36, 40, 43, 45, 48, 50, 57 above, 66, 71, 76, 78, 87, 92, 97); Cape Archives (12, 19, 22, 31, 61, 62, 83); Mr Esdon Frost (14, 15, 34 both); Kimberley Library (52, 55 both, 69); Local History Museum, Durban (57 below, 75, 121 below left); Mr H. W. Dickens, Kimberley (86); *Cape Times* (100, 107, 115 above, 131); *The Times,* London (103); State Information Office, Pretoria (105, 115 below); *The Argus,* Cape Town (110, 133, 135); *The Star,* Johannesburg (118, 121 above, centre and below right, 123, 125, 128 both, 129, 138).

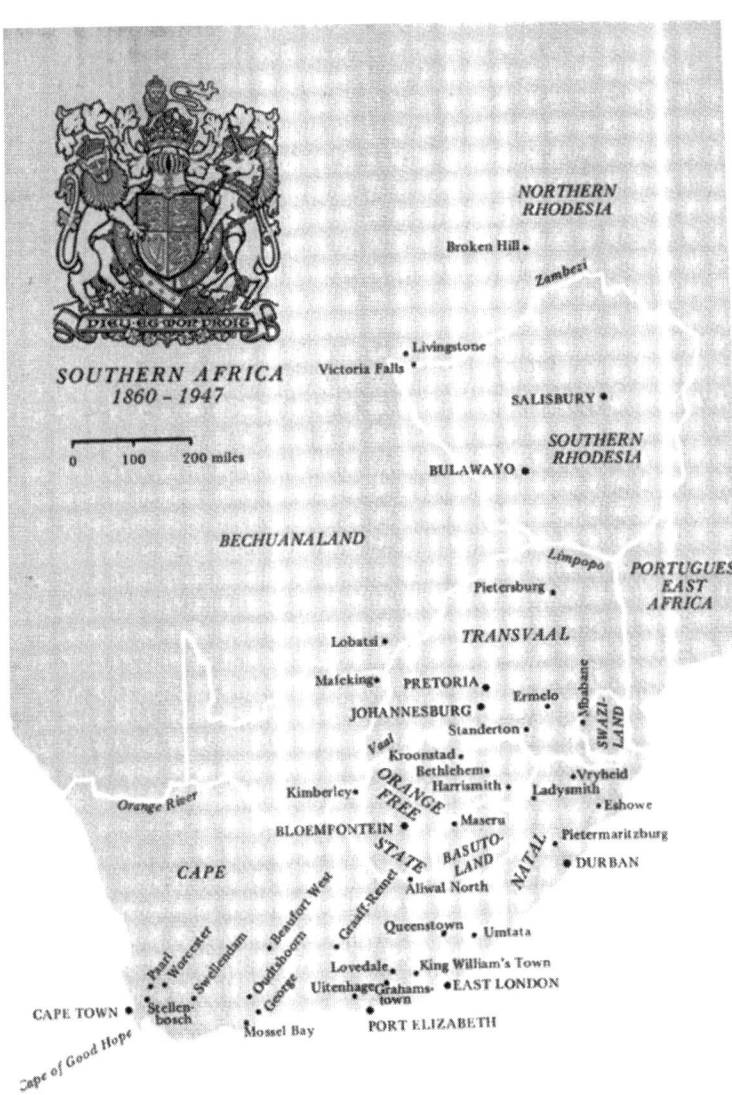

NORTHERN
RHODESIA

Broken Hill •

Zambezi

• Livingstone

SOUTHERN AFRICA
1860 – 1947

Victoria Falls •

SALISBURY •

0   100   200 miles

SOUTHERN
RHODESIA

BULAWAYO •

BECHUANALAND

Limpopo

PORTUGUES
EAST
AFRICA

Pietersburg •

Lobatsi •

TRANSVAAL

Mafeking•   PRETORIA •

Ermelo •

JOHANNESBURG •

Standerton •

Vaal   Kroonstad •

Orange River

Kimberley•

Bethlehem•
Harrismith •

ORANGE

Vryheid •

Ladysmith •

• Eshowe

FREE

BLOEMFONTEIN •

• Maseru

STATE   BASUTO-

Pietermaritzburg

• DURBAN

CAPE

LAND

Aliwal North

Beaufort West

Graaff-Reinet

NATAL

Queenstown   • Umtata

Paarl   Worcester

Swellendam

Oudtshoorn

George

Lovedale•   • King William's Town

Uitenhage Grahams-   • EAST LONDON

CAPE TOWN •   Stellen-
bosch

Cape of Good Hope

Mossel Bay

town

PORT ELIZABETH

ix

PREFACE

The title of this book indicates its approach. In dealing with the various British royalties who toured South Africa, I have tried to present them as something more than mere visitors: they are seen, rather, as ambassadors for the monarchy. To a certain extent, I have used these royal visits to explore the relationship between South Africa and the British Crown.

For this reason I have not included all royal visitors to South Africa. In the main, I have confined myself to official, as opposed to private, visits, and of these I have dealt only with the more important or more interesting ones. I have not, for instance, included the tour of Prince George, Duke of Kent, in 1934, for the reason that it was not particularly significant and that it would have meant covering very much the same ground as in the far more politically important tour undertaken by his brother, the Prince of Wales, a decade before.

Nor is this book concerned with the spells of duty of those royal governors-general, Prince and Princess

Arthur of Connaught, and the Earl and Countess of Athlone. I have confined myself to visitors only.

And, finally, this is not a detailed, day-by-day account of the various royal tours. Rather it is a series of biographical studies of the visitors themselves and an attempt to evaluate the mood and the political significance of these occasions.

I have received a great deal of help during the writing of this book, but my chief debt is to Mr Brian Roberts, whose interest, encouragement and extensive knowledge of South African history have proved invaluable. For further information, advice and assistance I must thank H.R.H. Princess Alice, Countess of Athlone; Mr Robert Mackworth Young of the Royal Library, Windsor Castle; Mr M. H. Buys of the Government Archives, Pretoria; Mrs Katherine Drake, Mrs B. Gosling and the staff of the South African Library, Cape Town; the staff of the Library of Parliament, Cape Town; Mr J. Smalberger of the Cape Archives; Mrs D. Strutt of the Local History Museum and Mr Dennis McCarthy of the Killie Campbell Africana Library, Durban; Mr A. Porter of the Port Elizabeth Library; Mrs F. van Niekerk and Mrs M. Macey of the Kimberley Library; Mrs Dorothy Caine of the Kommetjie Library; Mrs Miriam Bloomberg; Mrs Nora Hannah; Miss Marjorie Juta; Miss Norah Henshilwood; Mr Brocas Harris; Mr André Bothner; and Maurice and Judy Hoare, in whose home in Kimberley much of this manuscript was written.

For the use of short extracts I am deeply indebted to the authors and/or publishers of the following books: *Selected Correspondence 1884–1902* by Sir James Rose Innes (Van Riebeeck Society, Cape Town, 1972); *Boundless Privilege* by Marjorie Juta (Human & Rousseau, Cape Town, 1974); *The Royal Family in Africa* by Dermot Morrah (Hutchinson, London, 1947); *Queen Mary* by James Pope-Hennessy (George Allen & Unwin, London, 1959); *The Shadows Lengthen* by Piet van der Byl (Howard Timmins, Cape Town, 1973); *H.R.H.* by F. E. Verney (Hodder & Stoughton, London, n.d.); *A King's Story* by the Duke of Windsor (Cassell, London, 1951).

I must thank Her Majesty Queen Elizabeth II, by whose gracious permission the photograph of Prince Albert Victor and Prince George is here reproduced. Grateful acknowledgement is made to Burke's Peerage Limited for the illustration of the Royal Arms on the jacket.

For the use of pictures I am grateful also to Dr A. M. Lewin Robinson of the South African Library; Mrs D. Strutt of the Local History Museum and Mr Dennis McCarthy of the Killie Campbell Africana Library, Durban; the Cape Archives; the Government Archives; Mr H. W. Dickens of Kimberley; Mr Esdon Frost of Cape Town; the *Cape Times*; *The Argus*, Cape Town; and Mr Charles Barry and *The Star*, Johannesburg, who were particularly helpful.

Prince Alfred, Queen Victoria's sixteen-year-old son, painted by F.R. Say. Table Mountain appears, mistily, in the background.

PRINCE ALFRED

1

IT WAS A PITY THAT HE WAS SO SMALL. EVEN AT FIFTEEN, the year of his confirmation, Prince Alfred looked more like a boy of twelve or thirteen. He was, complained his mother Queen Victoria, 'very *short* for his age', although she imagined that he was less so than his elder brother Bertie had been at fifteen.

In other ways, though, Prince Alfred – or Affie – seemed to be something of an improvement on Bertie. Whereas the Prince of Wales was indolent, stubborn and slow to learn, Prince Alfred, who was three years younger, was active, alert and engagingly mannered. Indeed, it had been partly to get Affie away from Bertie's detrimental influence that the Queen and, more particularly, Prince Albert had earlier decided to separate the two boys. At the age of eleven, Prince Alfred had been packed off to live at Royal Lodge, Windsor, with a governor of his own. It was hoped that, under the benign but watchful eye of Major John Cowell, Affie would develop into a model prince: the sort of intelligent, enlightened and diligent son for which Prince Albert so ardently longed. Queen Victoria might lament the fact that sons were no longer one's own after the age of ten but she would never have dreamed of opposing her husband's highminded if somewhat cold-hearted scheme. With Bertie proving such a disappointment, they must do what they could to get the best out of Affie.

And they seemed to be getting it. Of the lethargy and backwardness of his elder brother, Prince Alfred was showing no trace. Major Cowell reported the boy to be quick-witted and eager to learn. As it had long ago been decided that Affie should go into the navy, he joined H.M.S. *Euryalus* as a midshipman in 1858. He was then fourteen. Queen Victoria, visiting him soon after he had reported aboard, was delighted to see him 'in his middle's jacket, cap, and dirk, half-blushing and looking very happy'. Her son might be disappointingly small but he was undeniably handsome – almost pretty – and full of spirit. Prince Albert, less effusive but no less proud, had in the meantime sent off the boy's excellent naval entrance-examination papers for the perusal of Lord Derby, the current Prime Minister.

Prince Affie at the time of his visit to South Africa.

The exacting father was no less pleased with his son's moral progress. 'Alfred', reported the Prince Corsort to his eldest daughter Vicky, 'fully recognises his personal responsibility for his own conduct and his own happiness.' At the time of Prince Alfred's confirmation, in April 1860, the Prince Consort treated the fifteen-year-old boy to one of his wordier and more erudite lectures on the 'struggle between the animal nature and the moral law'. The more matter-of-fact Queen contented herself by saying that she hoped her son 'should have as few failings as mortal man can have'.

It was a vain hope. As always, when it came to their dealings with their sons, the royal couple had set their sights too high. Affie might be brighter than Bertie but he was no paragon, neither of intellect nor of virtue. He was simply a lively, likable lad who would come, in time, to share most of his elder brother's regrettable but human weaknesses. Once at sea, Affie flung himself with gusto into the duties – and the diversions – of his fellow midshipmen. He was, as one observer put it, 'full of fun and life'. Major Cowell, who accompanied him to sea, could not watch him *all* the time. Even princes, it seems, were ready to sample traditional naval practices. 'For reasons which I cannot chronicle, but which referred to midshipman days,' wrote one scurrilous diarist in later years, the rakish Lord Charles Beresford always addressed Prince Alfred as 'darling Mathilda'. When Prince Alfred laughingly threatened to kick Lord Charles for this impertinent reminder of his boyhood indiscretions, the answer would be, 'You dare, and I'll show you up in the papers!'

Of any such improprieties, however, the serious-minded Prince Consort was mercifully unaware. One of his firmest resolves was that his sons should not go the way of Queen Victoria's wicked uncles. And not only must they lead more moral lives, but they must lead more useful ones. The days when princes could live in luxury, licentiousness and idleness were over; they must now earn the love and respect of the people. Prince Albert had long ago decided that, to best control the rising tide of democracy, it was necessary to breed a race of well-behaved, well-informed and hard-working royalties. A sense of royal dedication had become all-important. In what could well be termed the Coburg ideal of constitutional monarchy, the Crown must become a symbol of service.

Thus, when it was first suggested that the fifteen-year-old Prince Alfred go out to South Africa to inaugurate the proposed new breakwater in Table Bay at Cape Town, the Prince Consort was delighted. Already it had been agreed that Bertie, the Prince of Wales, should visit Canada to open the impressive new bridge across the St Lawrence at Montreal. The prospect of both his sons fulfilling these colonial engagements fired the Prince Consort's imagination. This was exactly the useful yet spectacular role which he envisaged for the members of the British royal house. It was the very thing to lift the monarchy high above the hurly-burly of everyday politics. The princes would become ambassadors, not so much for their country as for the Crown.

Queen Victoria in 1857

'What a cheering picture is here of progress and expansion of the British race and of the useful co-operation of the royal family in the civilisation which England has developed and advanced,' wrote Albert to Baron Stockmar, that equally highminded *éminence grise* of the Coburg family.

The London *Times* was no less enthusiastic about the idea. Such royal journeys would put an end to the traditional 'immobility' of British royalty.

The distressing 'narrowness' of Queen Victoria's Hanoverian predecessors had been due to their remaining 'within a certain radius of London'. Now, by these voyages to the British possessions across the seas, the princes would not only widen their own horizons but link the colonies more firmly to the mother country.

By the year 1860, the importance of such a link had not been given much thought. The imperial idea was still in its infancy. British imperialism, which during the following half-century was to develop into such a strident, swaggering and, in many ways, glorious ideal, was still a vague and suspect doctrine. The Empire was as yet a haphazard affair, a collection of widely scattered, widely varying and only loosely connected possessions, which a great many politicians were only too ready to scrap. The concept of this kaleidoscopic collection of British-run dependencies – ranging from isolated islands to vast continents – becoming one day united in loyalty to the British Crown seemed hardly feasible nor desirable.

Yet to the Prince Consort and his devoted wife the concept was beginning to make a considerable appeal. In an after-dinner speech at Trinity House, Prince Albert claimed that his sons could play a significant part 'in the development of those distant and rising countries who recognise in the British Crown and their allegiance to it their supreme bond of union with the mother country and with each other'.

Prince Albert

And so, in the summer of 1860, Queen Victoria's sons set off on their respective missions. The Prince of Wales sailed for Canada, and Prince Alfred for South Africa. Affie, admitted the Queen to her Uncle Leopold, King of the Belgians, 'was very low at going, though very happy to return to his ship'.

His lowness might well have been due not only to the fact that he was leaving home but to his being entrusted with so important a task. This slight, simple, fifteen-year-old boy would have the responsibility of carrying out the first royal visit to South Africa. One may be quite certain, however, that he was not going unprepared. He was to be accompanied by the vigilant Major Cowell and he would have been crammed, to bursting-point, with the Prince Consort's excellent, if unnerving, advice.

On 5 May 1860 H.M.S. *Euryalus* steamed out of Spithead, bound for the Cape. King Leopold, who must needs express an opinion on every subject, assured his niece Queen Victoria that Alfred's voyage to the Cape was a 'most wise measure'. South Africa, pronounced the Belgian King, 'has a great future to expect . . .'.

2

The harbour-master at Simonstown, coming alongside the *Euryalus* on the evening of 24 July 1860, was astonished to see Queen Victoria's son on duty at the gangway. Only on shore, it seems, was Prince Alfred to be treated as his mother's representative; while at sea, he continued with his duties as a midshipman.

The little naval base at Simonstown, however, was in no mood for such distinctions. Although Prince Alfred's visit was not due to start, officially, until the following morning, Simonstown was determined to begin the celebrations there and then. The town was loyally if somewhat amateurishly illuminated and the streets echoed with cheers. To the gratification of all, the Prince came ashore to spend the night with the Admiral's representative (the Admiral himself was away), but the visit was a private one and the youngster returned to his ship the following morning.

Things began in earnest at ten on the morning of Tuesday 25 July. It was a beautiful day. Although midwinter, the sun blazed from a blue and cloudless sky, setting the whole animated scene a-sparkle.

Simonstown, which was little more than a street of buildings wedged between the mountain and the sea, was looking its trim and whitewashed best. When Prince Alfred, in his simple midshipman's uniform, had clambered into the first of the line of carriages drawn up at Admiralty Pier, the cortège moved off in the direction of Cape Town, twenty-three miles away.

It was, as the *Cape Argus* never tired of pointing out to its readers, 'a truly royal progress'. With the sea glittering on its right and the mountains towering on its left, the procession rattled along the road that skirted a succession of creamy-coloured beaches. At the fishing-village of Kalk Bay, the party was joined by more carriages and riders. Still more riders fell in as the road swung away from the coast. Through an enchantingly wooded landscape, of oaks and pines and bluegums, enlivened by whitewashed walls and set against the great blue buttresses of Table Mountain, the ever swelling cavalcade moved on. At noon it reached the village of Claremont. Here were waiting the Governor, Sir George Grey, and the Lieutenant Governor, Major-General Wynyard. The greetings over, Prince Alfred exchanged his carriage for a horse and rode on towards Cape Town.

Cap in hand, bowing and smiling to left and right, the boy jogged along the ever more colourful and clamorous streets. Through one triumphal arch after another, beneath fluttering flags and rippling bunting, to the thunder of guns and the sea-like roar of the crowd, Alfred made his way towards the centre of the city. He could never have seen such a variety of people. Few other countries could rival the mixture of races that was the delight – and would ultimately be the dilemma – of South Africa. Their colours ranged, as one reporter put it, 'from the palest white to the deepest black'. There were Europeans of almost every nationality, but most of them British or Afrikaner descendants of the colonial Dutch; there were Africans and Coloured people and Hottentots and, most exotic of all, Malays with brilliant clothes and sleekly oiled hair.

A painting, by Thomas Bowler, of Prince Alfred riding in procession up Adderley Street, Cape Town.

And if the Prince was delighted by the variety and enthusiasm of the crowds, they were no less delighted by him. In his plain uniform and with his friendly bearing, he was, said one observer, 'just like any other frank, pleasant, high-bred young English gentleman . . . not a bit of a fop; not a bit of a milksop'.

On and on he rode, with the great sweep of Table Bay coming into view on the one hand, and the massive, flat-topped bulk of Table Mountain rising on the other. The little city into which Prince Alfred rode that winter's morning still retained a great deal of its late-eighteenth-and early-nineteenth-century flavour: its public buildings work simple classical façades and its private houses had high stoeps and shuttered windows. It was a place of considerable charm.

Reaching Adderley Street, which ran through the heart of the city, the procession turned and made for the avenue of winter-bare trees that led to Government House. But even here the Prince was not free of the applauding crowds, for the Botanical Gardens opposite Government House were crammed with specially invited spectators, and within the sprawling house itself was assembled a host of guests for that afternoon's levee.

That night, the Prince emerged once more into the streets. He was being taken to see the illuminations. If His Royal Highness had ever seen anything more spectacular, Cape Town had certainly not. A wealth of blazing bonfires, of soaring rockets, of dazzling roman candles and of colourful transparencies – each carrying a fervently loyal message – had transformed the little city into something of a fairyland.

That the hearts of his mother's subjects beat loyal and true, Prince Alfred could have been left in no doubt whatsoever.

But some hearts, of course, beat more loyal and true than others. Britain had ruled the Colony for over half a century, and to those Englishmen, living half a world away from their mother country, Prince Alfred's visit held a particular significance. 'And now,' pronounced the *Cape Chronicle*, 'to see him actually here among us, a member of that Royal Family which, to so large a proportion of our population, is a sort of myth or abstraction, brought with it an odd feeling of old recollections, and home longings, and a sense of dear old England, and all the greatness and nobleness which have as yet to be created in this distant corner of the world. . . .'

'The advent of a boy of fifteen to our shores is nothing;' continued the *Chronicle*, 'but as embodying in himself the power of England, manifesting itself in goodwill to us, it amounts almost to the sublime.'

If the imperial idea had not yet taken root in the heart of the Empire, it was certainly flourishing in its extremities.

3

With all these fervently expressed imperial sentiments, the Governor of the Cape, Sir George Grey, was in full agreement. Prince Alfred's visit was giving His Excellency's attitudes, and his *amour-propre*, a considerable boost.

As Governor of the Cape, Grey had inherited an extremely complicated situation. By the 1850s the British government, far from wanting to aggrandise the Empire, was thinking of ways of whittling it down. It was particularly anxious to wash its hands of its South African responsibilities. As always, the country was chock-a-block with problems. Thankfully, Britain had recently recognised the independence of the two Boer republics, the Transvaal and the Orange Free State – lying to the north of the Cape Colony – and it was determined that the Colony itself should become self-sufficient and self-defending. In addition, the tribes that were harassing the Colony's eastern frontier must be pacified. In fact peace, at practically any price, was all the British government wanted of its remaining South African possessions.

Sir George Grey

Sir George Grey, posted to the Cape in 1854, was quite the wrong man for the carrying out of this recessive policy. Charming, good-looking, humane, able, well-intentioned and idealistic, Grey had a mind of his own. He could be extremely pig-headed. Had this obstinacy and high-handedness been employed in the pursuance of the British government's policy, all would have been well, but on almost no point did Grey agree with Whicehall.

Whereas Britain wanted to separate the blacks from the whites on the eastern frontier and retain the tribal system, Grey was all for extending government control of the tribes and integrating them with the white colonists. Whereas Britain discouraged further European settlement in the eastern districts, Grey encouraged it. Whereas Britain was determined to cut down frontier expenditure, Grey increased it. And, most serious of all, whereas Britain wanted its interests confined, in the main, to Cape Town and Table Bay, Grey was following a defiant policy of expansionism. He was determined to bring about a federation of the Cape, Natal, the Transvaal and the Orange Free State. He was, in fact, the first British administrator to look upon South Africa as a single country.

Faced with Grey's defiant stand, the British government recalled him in 1859. But by the time the disgraced Governor reached England, there had been a change of government. He was reappointed. Grey was warned, however, that on no account was he to pursue his federal schemes. Disillusioned, he returned to the Cape. On the voyage back he became more disillusioned still, for he discovered that his wife, the lovely Lady Eliza Grey, was flirting with the captain. The infuriated Grey insisted that the ship turn back to dump the errant Eliza at Rio de Janeiro. Husband and wife remained estranged for the following thirty-seven years.

It was thus a frustrated, unhappy and disappointed man who arrived back in Cape Town in the middle of 1860.

There was only one ray of light to pierce the Governor's gloom: the forthcoming visit of Prince Alfred. It was in fact Grey who had instigated it. For years the Governor had been urging the building of a breakwater to render the notoriously dangerous Table Bay safer for shipping; while in England in 1859, he had suggested that Prince Alfred come out to grace the inaugural ceremony. Now, armed with the promise that the Queen's son would indeed attend the celebrations, Grey was able to chivvy the tardy Cape Parliament into going ahead with the scheme.

But there would be more to the Prince's visit than the mere inaugurating of the breakwater. Grey must have been fully alive to the potential of the occasion. For one thing, this first visit by a member of the royal family would lend some much-needed lustre to what had been, for the Governor, a disastrous term of office. Some of the glory was bound to be reflected onto him.

And, more important, could not the presence of the Prince – this symbol of the British Crown – be used to heal old wounds, to win friends, both black and white, and to draw attention to the virtues of Grey's own schemes? Could not the advent of this unsullied, disinterested, a-political figure serve to highlight the very highmindedness of Grey's federal policy? What Grey needed was *le grand geste:* something to dramatise, and symbolise, the desirability of a peaceful coming together of the various states and peoples of South Africa.

This would be Prince Alfred's role.

Was this why the Governor decided that, before inaugurating the breakwater in September, Prince Alfred should travel through the country; through, in fact, those very parts which had been such bones of contention between His Excellency and the British government? It looks very like it. For Sir George Grey had arranged for his royal guest to journey – not through the settled parts of the Cape Colony – but along the troubled eastern frontier, beside the borders of the no less troublesome Basutoland, across the Orange Free State, along the southern border of the Transvaal and down through Natal.

It was almost as though Prince Alfred's journey had been designed to link, by a fine royal thread, those areas which Sir George Grey had once planned to link in a more tangible fashion.

4

From the moment of his arrival at Government House, Affie was on the move. Dutifully the boy trudged through the Museum and the Castle and the Observatory and the Botanical Gardens. He visited wine farms, he received deputations, he presided at banquets, he attended reviews. He was entertained, in their gracious, gabled country houses, by leading colonial families – the Van Reenens, the Van der Byls and the Cloetes. Night after night he uncomplainingly guided the gratified matrons of Cape Town about the dance floor. Only a persistent mist – the famous 'tablecloth' – kept him from being taken up Table Mountain. And only occasionally did a welcome overstep what some considered to be the bounds of propriety. When Mathieson the hatter hung out a banner carrying the bold message 'Welcome, Royal Alfred, Who's Your Hatter?' he was severely taken to task by a leader writer on one of the newspapers.

For the rest, everyone was charmed. By his youth, his good looks, his unaffected manners and his air of enjoyment, Prince Alfred in no time won the hearts of the citizens of Cape Town. He had only to appear in the streets for there to be a concerted rush to catch a glimpse of him; he moved always in an aura of admiration.

But it was not, of course, the hearts of Cape Town's English population that Prince Alfred was obliged to win. He would have had those in any case. Less susceptible were those descendants of the original

Dutch settlers. The fact that Britain had occupied the Cape some fifty years before still rankled in the hearts of many Afrikaners; indeed, a great number of those in the outlying districts had packed up and left the Colony during the 1830s in order to found their own republics, the Transvaal and the Orange Free State. And those that had remained were still far from being reconciled to the administration.

Therefore, before taking the Prince to the eastern districts, Sir George Grey sent him to spend a few days in the heartland of these disaffected Afrikaners. The boy visited the towns of Paarl and Stellenbosch.

The journey took him through some of the loveliest scenery in the country: a well-watered, well-cultivated landscape of vineyards and orchards and long-established farms, all set against a background of magnificent mountains. The towns themselves, with their oak-lined streets and their whitewashed houses and their tranquil air, were the two prettiest in the Colony; and this despite the garish and hastily rigged up decorations to honour the royal visitor. Prince Alfred was given a surprisingly warm welcome. The Afrikaners were renowned for their hospitality and not even the most unresigned could long resist the boy's open countenance and friendly smile. Here was no arrogant and autocratic foreign princeling; merely a good-natured youngster set on enjoying every minute of his journey. He melted more hearts still when the story was told of how, on getting into bed in a Paarl hotel, the Prince discovered that his young travelling companion, midshipman Jocelyn, had stuffed his bed with walnuts and tangerines.

H.M.S. Euryalus

On Thursday 2 August, Prince Alfred returned to Simonstown. That afternoon, together with Sir George Grey and General Wynyard, he set sail in the *Euryalus* for Port Elizabeth and the Eastern Cape. His mission was about to start in earnest.

5

Prince Alfred arrived in Port Elizabeth, on 6 August 1860, with a heavy cold. It could hardly have been improved by the sight of an interminable poem of welcome, written by a Mr George Stow. Whether or not the boy read it one does not know, but the writer was assured that it 'had been laid before His

Royal Highness'. It was not the first, nor was it by any means to be the last, of the poems to be laid before the Prince. By the time he left South Africa, Prince Alfred was in possession of enough poor verse to fill a small library.

But a bad cold and a bad poem were not the only things to make memorable the Prince's arrival in Algoa Bay. The day marked his birthday – Affie turned sixteen that day. The citizens of Port Elizabeth could therefore feel themselves doubly blessed: they could celebrate a royal visit and a royal birthday at one stroke.

Port Elizabeth, lying some five hundred miles along the coast from Cape Town, had been officially established for about forty years. Its atmosphere was quite different from that of Cape Town. It was more like a small English or Scottish seaport, bustling, wind-swept and close-packed, with its flat-fronted houses crowding the stony hillsides above the sea. Today, of course, it was all a-flutter. The Prince was to spend only a day and a night in the town but its residents were determined that he should miss not one notable sight. In 'boisterous' weather, the boy was driven through the crowded streets (spanned by the inevitable triumphal arches, one sporting bales of wool), shown over the Grey Institute for Boys, the new hospital, the new prison, the still unfinished Town Hall and the preparations for that evening's ball to be held in the 'spacious premises of the P.E. Boating Company'.

The tour of inspection over, he enjoyed an hour's riding. Prince Alfred was being accommodated in the town's most imposing residence, the home of Mr William Fleming, and it was here that the leading citizens had the honour of dining with the Prince. Never, the boy assured his gratified listeners in a short after-dinner speech, would he forget the birthday that he had spent in Port Elizabeth. Then, cold or no cold, the Prince was whisked off to the ball.

Prince Alfred's visit to Port Elizabeth brought forth at least one amusing, if apocryphal, anecdote. Making polite conversation with a certain Mrs Kettle, the Prince asked if her children were boys or girls. Boys, answered an ebullient Mrs Kettle; all her little kettles, she added roguishly, had spouts.

6

Forsaking his midshipman's uniform for something more suitable – a hunting-outfit, complete with top boots and a helmet – Prince Alfred set off from Port Elizabeth on the morning of 7 August. For the following four weeks his party, which included the Governor, would be travelling overland.

The 1,200-mile journey, from Port Elizabeth to Durban, via the Orange Free State, would be made by wagon and on horseback. Most nights Prince Alfred, together with his companion, midshipman Jocelyn, would sleep in a tented wagon. It was to be a journey of great variety, of men, animals, scenery and climate. Prince Alfred was to meet Britons, Boers, Xhosas,

Fingos, Hottentots, Basutos and Zulus. He would see all manner of game, from ostriches to wildebeest. He would ford rivers and cross mountains and canter through the seemingly endless veld. He would experience bitter cold, scorching sunshine and enervating humidity.

Never once did he complain; never once was his behaviour less than admirable. In whatever respects Affie may, or may not, have resembled his parents, he had inherited their Coburg sense of duty, of royal obligation towards others. All duties expected of him were carried out with great aplomb and apparent enjoyment.

'Nothing', wrote Sir George Grey in a private letter to a friend, 'can be more gratifying than everything connected with Prince Alfred's journeys here. He is a noble young fellow, full of life and fun. He is received everywhere with transports of delight. He rides as far and fast as I can myself, delights in every style of life, wins the hearts of all the native chiefs, gladdens the Europeans by the interest he takes in their prosperity, and by the good influence he exercises over the natives, as also by turning out in dress and even minute articles of equipment a thorough South African sportsman.'

His naturalness, his verve, his lack of all hauteur, never ceased to charm and astonish. Only occasionally, and then in the most good-natured way possible, did any sign of his royal status reveal itself. When, at a ball in some country town, a lady asked after 'his mother', Affie replied that 'Her Majesty the Queen' was quite well. And at yet another ball, when an over-excited young lady kept addressing him as 'My Highness', the Prince naughtily led her on to repeat the *faux pas* for the amusement of the rest of his party.

The first stay, after Port Elizabeth, was made in Grahamstown, 'which prides itself on being the most thoroughly English town in South Africa'. Here Affie attended a grandiloquently termed *fête champêtre*, given by the recently knighted Sir Walter Currie at his home, 'Oatlands'. From Grahamstown the party moved into what was known as British Kaffraria – the frontier district which had not long ago been the scene of bitter fighting between black and white. It was with these green and rolling uplands that Sir George Grey was so deeply concerned: its pacification, civilisation and integration with the rest of the Colony was one of the Governor's dearest wishes.

To isolated British communities – at Alice, Fort Beaufort, King William's Town and Queenstown – the sight of Queen Victoria's son afforded immense cheer and reassurance. His health was drunk in lonely farmhouses; he was hailed by little garrisons in makeshift forts; the strains of 'God Save the Queen', sung by Coloured girls at mission stations, were carried away on the thin winter wind. In great masses, tribesmen gathered to pay him homage.

Prince Alfred stands beside his travelling-wagon (with the royal coat of arms). At his feet lies a wildebeest which he has just shot.

'They charged down upon the party in imposing barbaric native fashion,' runs one report, 'shouting their war cry, and shaking their assegais until they came within forty yards of the spot where His Royal Highness stood to receive them.'

'We have seen the Child of Heaven; we have seen the Son of our Queen,' they would shout. And if it all sounded a little sacrilegious, no one grumbled.

Not far from Queenstown the Prince met up with the once powerful Xhosa chief, Sandile. Humbled since the war with the British of a decade before, Sandile and his counsellors now came to pay their respects to Queen Victoria's son. 'They were in strange guise enough,' complained one observer, 'and in their partial adoption of European habiliments, seemed more *outré* than if dressed, or undressed, in the barbaric simplicity of their native costume.'

But suitably dressed or no, Sandile was invited by Prince Alfred to accompany him, on the *Euryalus,* when he returned to the Cape. Sir George Grey no doubt imagined that Sandile would be impressed, not only by this mark of royal favour but by the wonders of British civilisation, both on the *Euryalus* and at Cape Town. Overcoming his reluctance, Sandile accepted. The chief and his counsellors would board the ship at Port Elizabeth, sail in her to Durban, and there await the arrival of the Prince.

If Sandile was willing to put his faith in the British, his people were not, 'Sandile's tribe begged him with tears as he passed not to trust himself in our hands,' reported Major Cowell to the Prince Consort, 'for they knew that he would be executed, and the fact of the Rev. Tya Toga accompanying him only increased this belief in his fate, for they said that we always employ a clergyman on such occasions.' But Sandile went.

At Aliwal North, on the border between the Cape Colony and the Orange Free State, Prince Alfred met another renowned chieftain, Moshweshwe, or Moshesh as he was known to his British contemporaries. For years this astute Basuto chieftain had been a thorn in the side of Sir George Grey; there was constant friction between the Basutos and the Boers of the Orange Free State, with Grey being obliged to act as mediator. At the moment there was a state of uneasy peace between Britain, Boer and Basuto.

On being told that Queen Victoria's son would be passing through Aliwal North, Moshweshwe gathered three hundred of his followers and came galloping down from his mountain kingdom to greet him. In a swirl of dust, his cavalcade poured through the Nek – the pass in a range of hills – and halted before the oncoming royal party. The old chief removed his top hat; Prince Alfred removed his helmet and extended his hand. With the unnerving sound of assegais being rattled against hide shields reverberating in his ears, the Prince accepted a letter from Moshweshwe. The chief asked him to present it to the Queen. It was a request for an alliance with Britain. Affie, in turn, gave Moshweshwe a portrait of himself.

The formalities over, the Prince and the chieftan went riding side by side into Aliwal North.

7

On Monday 20 August, the Prince's party splashed across the Orange River and rode into the Orange Free State. Since the British recognition of its independence, half a dozen years before, the Orange Free State was once more a republic with a president and a volksraad of its own. This was a fact which not all the country's British residents were happy to accept. Indeed, the visit of Prince Alfred gave them a splendid opportunity to reaffirm their loyalty and, no less important, to air their dissatisfaction. There was a distinctly truculent note to some of their messages of welcome. 'We love him. *He is our Prince.* His mother is *our* Queen,' claimed the headline of one English newspaper, while on a banner were blazoned the words, 'Loyal, though discarded.'

But, for all this, the Prince was given a vociferous welcome. As the party jogged across the wide, open grasslands, bands of young men, their slouch hats trimmed with ostrich feathers, and their saddlecloths pricked out in red, white and blue, came galloping out of every village to meet him. The self-appointed escort from Bloemfontein, the little capital, was particularly lively. This band was known locally as the 'Dirty Boys' Corps'; not, one writer hastened to explain, because they were either unwashed or 'morally corrupt', but because of their 'exuberant flow of animal, with probably, now and then, a small admixture of ardent, *spirits*'. In truth, he stoutly maintained, they were 'the *young chivalrous manhood* of the Town'.

Be that as it may, the Dirty Boys fell in behind the Prince as, on a splendid grey horse, he came riding into Bloemfontein. That the capital of the Orange Free State – despite the triumphal arches, flags, banners, bunting and *feu-de-joie* from the cannon at the fort – was still little more than a village was underlined by the fact that, as the distinguished visitors entered at one end, so did a herd of wild buck enter at the other. The buck were hastily rounded up on the Market Square.

Moshoeshoe and some of his advisers in 1860,
on the occasion of Prince Alfred's visit.

Game, in fact, was to play a major part in Affie's
stay in the Orange Free State. The territory was
teeming with wild life. On the day after his arrival
in Bloemfontein, he attended a *grande battue* at
Hartebeestehoek, or Bain's Vlei, the farm of Andrew
Hudson Bain. An officer in attendance on the Prince
described it as 'that glorious day when we killed six
hundred head of game, all larger than horses', while
another writer claimed that it was 'doubtful whether
a hunt exceeding or even equalling in proportions
. . . ever took place in the present century as this

gigantic *Chase*'. He put the final tally at one thousand head of game.

It was, indeed, a slaughter on the most massive, crude and indiscriminate scale. A host of Africans ('yelling Kaffirs') had been detailed to drive the animals, of almost every variety, towards the homestead. As far as one could see through the great clouds of dust, the entire plain was a moving mass of game. Mounted on horses, the Prince and his companions fired into these bewildered and stampeding herds. Little Prince Alfred, shooting as fast as the guns could be loaded and handed to him, was credited with having shot some twenty-five head of game. 'Most of the sportsmen looked more like butchers than sportsmen from being so covered with blood,' wrote one exhilarated participant. 'His Royal Highness [was] red up to the shoulders from using the spear. . . .'

The excitement over, Affie returned to Bloemfontein for the night. On the following morning he resumed his journey. Now they were travelling north-east across the wide landscape, towards Winburg and the southern boundary of the Transvaal. Just outside Winburg, the party met up with Marthinus Pretorius, the President of the Orange Free State (the acting-President had received the Prince in Bloemfontein), who was returning from the Transvaal. As was everyone, Pretorius was charmed by the unaffected boy; when Affie presented his splendid travelling-wagon as a souvenir of his journey to the state, Pretorius – imagining that it had been presented to him personally – was more charmed still.

From Winburg, Prince Alfred travelled east, parallel to the Transvaal border, through Sandriver and Harrismith and finally down Van Reenen's Pass into Natal. Everywhere he was received with 'great enthusiasm and sundry addresses of welcome'.

By few was this show of enthusiasm for the son of the British sovereign more appreciated than by Sir George Grey. 'I have always felt it my duty, by every means in my power,' he took care to remind the inhabitants of the country, 'to promote the interests of the Orange Free State, feeling that in doing this I should be fulfilling the anxious wishes of the Queen.'

Whether Queen Victoria was as anxious to 'promote the interests' of the Orange Free State as Sir George Grey claimed, is a moot point; but there can be little doubt that she would have approved of his dreams of bringing it back into the imperial fold.

8

Of the loyalty of Natal to the British connection there was no flicker of doubt. Having crossed the Drakensberg mountains, Prince Alfred moved south through the lush valleys of sub-tropical Natal in an atmosphere of frenzied acclaim. The Boers, who had once planned to make Natal their home, had since packed up and left in the face of British encroachment; few of the Europeans in Natal were not now heart and soul for Britain. During the coming hundred years,

Natal was to remain the most staunchly and unques-
tioningly pro-British of the South African territories:
a faithful outpost of Empire, a semi-tropical suburbia.
Even the banners of welcome were the most fervent
yet encountered by the Prince. 'Thou royal, we loyal,'
proclaimed one; 'True Blue never stains,' announced
another. Only occasionally did a note of crass com-
mercialism temper this air of heady adoration, as in
'Welcome, Prince Alfred, Saker's Hotel'.

It was, however, by the indigenous population
– the Zulu – that Prince Alfred was given his first,
and most colourful, welcome. On coming down Van
Reenen's Pass ('through the back door', grumbled
the citizens of Durban) Affie was met by a host of
gleaming, chanting, stamping, assegaiwielding warriors, all intent on paying homage to the son of the
Great White Queen. The power of the once mighty
Zulu nation had been temporarily broken; the obese
and lethargic Zulu King Mpande now ruled his country by the grace of Britain.

In Pietermaritzburg, the little capital of the
Colony, the welcome took on a more conventional
flavour (although here, too, the Prince was entertained by a display of Zulu war-dancing) and Affie
did the usual round. He could spend only one day,
Tuesday 4 September, in the capital but it was a day of
relentless activity. He laid the foundation stone of the
new Town Hall, he planted a tree, he held a levee at
Government House, he presented new colours to the
85th Regiment, he sat his horse at a military review,

he watched those Zulu war-dances, he attended a mammoth ball in a specially erected building in the centre of the town.

It must all have been exhausting. Small wonder that one observer could note that 'the general expression pervading the features was that of gentleness and pensiveness, in part, no doubt, due to physical fatigue'.

Nevertheless, by eight the following morning, Affie had started his ride down the fifty-mile-long road that led, past the spectacular Valley of a Thousand Hills, to the port of Durban. Just beyond the village of Pinetown a handsome triumphal arch, 'profusely decorated with flags and ribbons, sugar cane, bananas, pineapples and flowers', came crashing to the ground, leaving only enough time for the widely flung materials to be arranged 'in the most graceful manner possible at the side of the road' before the royal party jogged by.

Durban, with its sandy streets and its verandahed houses and its palms and flamboyants and frangipani, was quite different from the other South African towns that Prince Alfred had seen. But here, too, he could afford to spend only a day and a night: the *Euryalus,* having sailed on from Port Elizabeth, was already anchored in the wide and beautiful bay. The Prince was accommodated in an hotel on the Market Square (its name was promptly changed to the 'Royal Hotel') and his appearance on its balcony led to a frenzied outburst of cheering from the crowd

outside. 'They cheered Prince Alfred, they cheered
the Queen, they cheered Prince Albert, they cheered
the royal children and then they started cheering
each of them all over again.'

That night found Affie partnering the inevitable
mayoress at the inevitable ball (this one held in Mr
Acutt's 'capacious suite of rooms') but his doctor
would not allow the still-exhausted boy to stay long.
Indeed, after that one dance with the ecstatic mayoress, he left.

But the climax of the Prince's stay in Natal was
yet to be enacted. On the morning of 6 September
he boarded the only train in South Africa. It carried him for the entire length of its track, two miles,
from the centre of Durban to the Point, off where
the *Euryalus* lay waiting. 'Away we went on the fastest
journey which African soil has yet seen,' wrote one of
the party; the journey took, in fact, the record time
of two minutes and forty seconds. 'Whatever festivities Prince Alfred may get at Cape Town when he
returns,' ran one smug comment, 'he at all events
won't get another railway trip. That is a feature of his
visit strictly Natalian.'

At six that evening the *Euryalus* weighed anchor
and steamed out of Durban Bay, bound once more
for Simonstown.

Aboard the *Euryalus* were the Xhosa chief Sandile
and his counsellors. It was with considerable relief
that the tribesmen saw Prince Alfred come aboard for,
as Major Cowell had reported to the Prince Consort,

'some had misgivings as to the real intentions of our Government'. Their relief turned to wonder when the following morning, with the ship at sea, they saw 'a number of hardy barefooted lads assisting at daybreak washing the decks, foremost among whom in activity and energy was the son of the Queen of England'.

In a touching letter to the captain of the *Euryalus,* Sandile afterwards made reference to this sense of wonderment. 'Up to this time,' he said, 'we have not ceased to be amazed at the wonderful things we have witnessed, and which are beyond our comprehension. But one thing we understand, the reason of England's greatness. When the son of her great Queen becomes subject to a subject, that he may learn wisdom . . . we see why the English are a great and mighty nation.'

9

On Monday 17 September 1860 came the highlight of Prince Alfred's South African visit: he inaugurated the new breakwater in Table Bay. The occasion, afterwards captured by those two talented artists Thomas Bowler and Thomas Baines, was one of exceptional brilliance. It was a showery, blustery day, with sudden shafts of sunlight to set the whole scene shimmering. In the background Table Mountain, with its attendant peaks, Lion's Head and Devil's Peak, were shrouded in mist, but the shoreline was alive with streaming flags, shifting crowds, kaleidoscopic uniforms, picturesque Malays, scurrying equerries, restive acrses and drifts of smoke from saluting cannon out on the foaming sea tossed scores of craft, from tiny rowing boats to towering warships, all fluttering with pennants.

Prince Affie tips the first load for the new breakwater.

The sun burst out as the Prince, with the Governor and their suites, came cantering up. They alighted at a little pavilion. From this pavilion a length of track led to the end of a wooden pier. When the salutes had been fired and the National

Anthem sung and a prayer offered up Prince Alfred followed a truck, piled high with rocks, along the jetty. With the truck in position at the end of the pier. the boy pullet the cord attached to a silver trigger. The truck tilted and sent its load of rocks splashing into the sea below. At this, the watching crowd raised a deafening shout and the ships at sea fired off their salvoes. It had all, apparently, been a tremendous triumph.

The painting, by Thomas Bowler, of the inauguration of the breakwater.

Prince Alfred had one more important duty to fulfil before he left the Cape. On the following day he inaugurated yet another of Sir George Grey's schemes: he opened the graceful new building of the South African Library and Museum in the Botanical Gardens.

On Wednesday 19 September Prince Alfred sailed away. It was, for those thousands upon thousands who crowded the shore to see him go, a poignant moment. More poignant still it became as the band of the *Euryalus* struck up that most heart-catching of melodies, 'Auld Lang Syne'. That this small, smiling and sweet-natured boy had captured the imagination of the colonists there was no doubt. 'At first our hearts opened to receive him for his *mother's* sake;' wrote one observer, 'now he sits enthroned in their inmost recesses for his own.'

Prince Alfred arrived back at Windsor early in November 1860. The Queen was delighted to welcome him home. 'Here', wrote Queen Victoria to her Uncle Leopold on 13 November, 'we have the happiness of having our dear Alfred back since the 9th, who gives *very* interesting accounts of his expedition, and has brought back *many* most interesting trophies, splendid horns of *all* those wonderful animals, photographs etc. . . . Major Cowell gives are *excellent* report of him in *every way* which, as you will readily believe, makes us *very* happy. He is really such a dear, gifted, handsome child. . . .'

10

The memory of Prince Alfred's visit lingered long after he had sailed away. Although he paid several more visits to South Africa in the course of his naval career, none was as long, nor as significant, as this first one. Looked back on, it seemed an almost euphoric period. 'Even those who took part in the receptions speak of them as the happiest days in their lives,' wrote someone in later years. 'They were weeks of uninterrupted happiness, one great general holiday-making that lasted for about a quarter of a year. There was neither work nor care. Every shop, place of business, and public office in the towns the Prince entered was closed. We never knew how the bills were paid at that time; nor how our daily bread was provided, neither bakers nor bankers ever appeared to be at business. . . . We promised, at his farewell, never to forget him, and he pledged us his eternal love and rememberance.'

The Duke of Edinburgh

The Duchess of Edinburgh

Affie's name lived on, not only in those acres of bad verse, but in such place names as Port Alfred and Prince Alfred's Hamlet, in the names of districts, streets, docks, regiments, songs, marches and innumerable mansions, villas and cottages. For years his birthday was kept as a public holiday and celebrated with balls and reviews and the firing of salutes. 'He has always said', it was claimed, 'that he considers himself more identified with South Africa than with any other part of the Colonial Empire.'

To this remote, unimportant Colony, Prince Alfred's visit had brought a breath of another, more brilliant and deeply rooted world; an assurance – to the British colonists at least – that they had not been forgotten by the mother country. 'We are part and parcel of this great and glorious fabric,' trumpeted the *Cape Chronicle,* 'but, as we live at a distance from the centre, we might fancy we are overlooked. To assure us that we are not so – that the heart beats responsive to the extremities – the Queen has sent her son to visit us. By doing so she has doubly cemented us to her.'

But Affie's visit had a deeper significance. His appeal (as Sir George Grey was quick to realise) was not only to the British colonists. Hitherto all Britain's representatives in South Africa had been political appointments. Now here was someone who stood above party politics, a direct link between the people and the Crown, between, moreover, *all* the people. It was one of the first manifestations of a new, particularly Victorian and imperial ideal. The conception of the Great White Queen – of a monarch of all the peoples of the Empire – was only just beginning, but Prince Alfred's visit to South Africa was an expression of this. Sir George Grey's assurance that the Prince 'carries away with him the heartiest good wishes of all ranks, races, creeds and colours in South Africa' was not all rhetoric. And on the day that Affie left, a plump Coloured woman was heard to shout, as she shoved her way through the crowds to get a better look at him, 'He is *my* Prince, too!' Her claim was not without significance.

11

No more than any of their sons did Prince Alfred (created Duke of Edinburgh in 1865) live up to his parents' high expectations. Indeed, in a very short time he was hurrying down his brother Bertie's paths of pleasure. In the year 1874 he married the only daughter of Tsar Alexander II of Russia, a somewhat bizarre alliance that was to have a still more bizarre sequence, for one of their daughters became that most conceited, expansive and theatrical of twentieth-century sovereigns, Queen Marie of Romania. In 1893 Prince Alfred succeeded to the dukedom of (as far as Queen Victoria was concerned) the most precious of duchies, Saxe-Coburg and Gotha. He died, in Coburg, at the age of fifty-five, in 1900, and while the aged Queen Victoria bemoaned his passing, her ladies-in-waiting whispered darkly about the 'intemperance' that had led to his untimely death.

It was all a far, far cry from the days when, as a fresh-faced boy, Affie had gone cantering across the tawny veld.

And Sir George Grey's plans for a South African Federation? They never materialised. Or rather, the idea of federation was shelved for a couple of decades. Not until almost twenty years after Prince Alfred's visit was the idea revived. This attempt proved to be no more successful than the last. And, once again, the collapse of the federal scheme coincided with a royal visit.

*The apathetic Prince Albert Victor (Eddy) and the lively
Prince George, at the time of their visit to South Africa.*

PRINCE EDDY
AND PRINCE GEORGE

1

O N ONE THING QUEEN VICTORIA'S ELDEST SON, THE prince of Wales, was resolved. His children would not be subjected to as rigorous an upbringing as he had been. His childhood, under the Prince Consort's idealistic but unimaginative guidance, had been a nightmare. His children must be spared that. With this resolve, the Princess of Wales – the chic, exquisite and feather-brained Princess Alexandra – was in full accord. She would, in any case, have been temperamentally incapable of inaugurating or sticking to any such scheme. Life, as far as the Prince and Princess of Wales were concerned, was for living. Both liked few things so much as to be surrounded by happy faces. And however wide Bertie might range in search of these happy faces, Alexandra was content to see them in her own home. Thus the five Wales children – two boys and three girls – were being raised in the most informal and indulgent fashion. If they did not run exactly wild, they certainly – by the standards of the time – ran very free.

They also ran very immature. Their mother was determined that they would remain as childlike as possible for as long as possible. So enduringly youthful herself, in both looks and personality, Princess Alexandra saw to it that her children did not grow up too quickly. It was as though mother and children lived in a make-believe world, in a state of eternal youth. To the Wales children their mother – so gay, so spontaneous, so impractical and unpunctual – was a delightful companion, hardly more grown-up than themselves. They called her 'darling Motherdear'.

Not all of this, however, could sufficiently explain the backwardness of the eldest son, Prince Albert Victor, known in the family as Eddy. Born, prematurely, in 1864, Prince Eddy had been subnormal from infancy. It was not that he was an imbecile; he was merely slow-witted. Throughout his boyhood he remained apathetic, listless, slow to react and quite unable to concentrate his attention on anything for long. When he made the effort, he could be charming, but making the effort was something which Prince Eddy was very loth to do.

His brother, Prince George, was different. Some eighteen months younger than Eddy, George (the future King George V) was a lively, intelligent and good-natured boy. He might be no more bookish, imaginative nor mature than Eddy or his three sisters, but he was steady and well-meaning. He was also devoted to his beautiful mother; in many ways, the two of them were more like sister and brother than mother and son.

The two princes were being educated together. Their tutor was the young Rev. John Dalton. It had taken Dalton very little time to realise that, without the presence of Prince George, Prince Eddy would achieve even less than he was doing; or that the more the boys were kept clear of what Dalton tactfully called the 'excitement' of their parents' lives, the better they would fare. On this second score, the princes' grandmother, Queen Victoria, needed no convincing. For year after year, for decade after decade, in season and out, Queen Victoria expressed her disapproval of the frivolous sort of life that was being led by the Prince and Princess of Wales. Thus when, in 1877, with Eddy thirteen and George eleven, Dalton suggested that they be sent away from home to continue their education, the Queen (for it was she who had to sanction any family plans) was all agreement.

It had long ago been decided that Prince George, as the second son, would join the navy. Had not his uncle Alfred, also a second son, been the Sailor Prince? Dalton now suggested that Prince Eddy accompany his brighter brother on the naval training-ship, the *Britannia*. 'Prince Albert Victor', reported Dalton to the Queen, 'requires the stimulus of Prince George's company to induce him to work at all. . . . The mutual influence of their characters on one another (totally different as they are in many ways) is very beneficial. . . .

Difficult as the education of Prince Albert Victor is now, it would be doubly or trebly so if Prince George were to leave him. Prince George's lively presence is his mainstay and chief incentive to exertion. . . .'

Queen Victoria could not at first agree to the plan. She had, she protested, 'a great fear of young and carefully brought up Boys mixing with older Boys and indeed with any Boys in general, for the mischief done by bad boys and the things they may hear and learn from them cannot be overrated'.

She was also afraid that a nautical education – as far as the heir presumptive was concerned – would foster too much national pride. A ruler, she explained (and here one hears the dying echoes of the Prince Consort's plan for that race of enlightened princes), should be above the prides and prejudices of narrow patriotism.

But in the end, for she was never as intransigent as many imagined, Queen Victoria gave way. Eddy and Georgie would go to sea together, 'as an experiment'.

The experiment lasted for two years. At the end of it, when Eddy was fifteen and a half and George fourteen, the situation had not much altered. Prince Eddy was in no way improved; he remained lethargic and backward. The only remedy that Dalton could suggest was more of the same: Eddy must accompany Georgie on another ship, H.M.S. *Bacchante,* for a series of cruises. With them would go Mr Dalton, a couple of other instructors and a cast of hand-picked lieutenants, sub-lieutenants, midshipmen and cadets – all of 'irreproachable character'.

With this plan, the Queen was no more pleased than she had been with the first but, once again, she bowed to the urgings of the Prince of Wales and Mr Dalton.

The two princes spent almost three years on the *Bacchante*. Their first cruise took them to the Mediterranean and the West Indies. Their second to Ireland and Spain. Their third, and longest, to South America, South Africa, Australia, Japan, China, Singapore and Egypt. While poor Eddy was kept to his books, Georgie was treated (as his Uncle Affie had been treated before him) like any other midshipman. The brothers shared a cabin, ate with the other midshipmen and cadets, and were accorded no special treatment. The scrappy and ill-spelt diaries kept by the boys were converted by the diligent Mr Dalton into a mammoth, learned and sanctimonious work, well larded with Latin quotations and moral maxims, entitled *The Cruise of H.M.S.* Bacchante. A more tedious book one could not hope to read. Of the pale, torpid and slow-witted Eddy or the suntanned, merry and quick-witted Georgie, hardly a trace is to be found in its 1,400 pages.

These cruises were broken of course by short visits ashore, by longer holidays at home (during which Queen Victoria would bombard the Prince of Wales with instructions that his sons be kept away from 'the society of fashionable and fast people') and by one long stay ashore, lasting seven weeks. This stay was made at the Cape of Good Hope, from 16 February to 9 April 1881.

2

British imperialism, during the years since Prince Alfred's visit to South Africa twenty years before, had burgeoned most spectacularly. It had developed into something far more self-conscious and self-confident, a combination of self-interest with idealism, of aggressiveness with humanitarianism, of covetousness with an almost mystical sense of dedication. It was part brute force, part highmindedness, part glory. Queen Victoria, coaxed out of her long period of mourning by the flamboyant Disraeli, had become an unquestionably imperial figure, the plump and imperious Queen-Empress of the jumble of peoples and territories that went to make up the greatest Empire that the world had ever known.

In South Africa, this imperial thrust had taken the form of yet another scheme for federation. The British Colonial Secretary, Lord Carnarvon, flushed with his success in uniting the various states of Canada under the British Crown, was determined to do the same for South Africa. He envisaged one great British dominion stretching from the Cape of Good Hope to the Limpopo, or even the Zambezi. Carnarvon's motives might not have been quite as elevated as Grey's (the fact that both diamonds and gold had by now been discovered in South Africa had given his imperialism a distinct shot in the arm) but he pursued his aim with more vigour. He disseminated propaganda, he soft-soaped the wary Boer republics, he called conferences, he pushed a South Africa Act through the British Parliament, he appointed a fervent imperialist as High

Commissioner and Governor of the Cape Colony. In 1877 he despatched the Governor of Natal, backed up by a handful of policemen, to annex the impoverished, bemused and demoralised Transvaal. Two years later the British broke the power of the revitalised Zulu nation and arrested their king Cetshwayo.

H.M.S. Bacchante, *with the princes on board, under full sail.*

But, in the end, the whole project misfired. Carnarvon's strong-arm tactics had not had the support of the Cape Colonial government, and the Zulu War, although technically a victory, had cost Britain dear in men and money. And then in December 1880 the Transvaal Boers, shaking off their lethargy, repudiated the annexation of their country and proclaimed a republic. Warming to their task, they besieged the various British garrisons in the Transvaal and galloped south to prevent any relieving force from entering from Natal.

The *Bacchante,* with Prince Eddy and Prince George aboard, was at the Falkland Islands, off the tip of South America, when news came of the Boer uprising. The Detached Squadron, with which the *Bacchante* was sailing, was ordered to head for the Cape instead of rounding the Horn as planned. 'We are going to the Cape of Good Hope,' noted Prince George in his diary for 26 January 1881, adding, with a touching ignorance of both situation and spelling, 'because of the Basuter disturbances'.

Queen Victoria was appalled to hear that the Detached Squadron had been diverted to the Cape. She was more appalled still to learn that her grandsons might be sent to the front with a special naval brigade. It was less than two years since the Bonapartist pretender, the young Prince Imperial, had been killed fighting for the British in the Zulu War; the Queen was not prepared to risk a repeat of any such tragedy in *her* family.

'I must earnestly protest', she telegraphed to the Prince of Wales, 'against the Princes serving with the Naval Brigade on shore at the Cape. I strongly objected to their both going to sea, but consented on the suggestion that it was necessary for their education. The proposal to send them on active service destroys the cause of my former consent, and there is no reason for, and many against, their incurring danger in the South African war.'

The Queen backed up this telegram with an unequivocal instruction to the First Lord of the Admiralty. The princes were not to be attached to any naval brigade. She trusted that, in future, the First Lord of the Admiralty would give no orders without first consulting her, 'so that the disagreement of opinions may not occur again'.

'The *Bacchante* going to the Cape,' she informed the boys' mother, Princess Alexandra, 'which was done in a hurry without due consultation with me (I disapproved) and feeling how valuable these two *young* lives are to the *whole Nation*, I felt *bound* to protect them against useless and unnecessary exposure in a cruel *Civil War*, for so it is, the Boers being *my subjects*, and it being a rule that Princes of the Royal Family *ought not* to be mixed up in it.'

But fulminate as she might, the Queen could not prevent the *Bacchante* from sailing to South Africa. On 16 February 1881, with the Boers (admittedly a good thousand miles away) barring any British advance

from Natal into the Transvaal, and the Cape Colony
in an uproar, the *Bacchante* arrived at Simonstown.

3

Unlike their uncle Alfred, Eddy and George had not
come to South Africa on an official visit. And Queen
Victoria, who always knew her own mind perfectly,
had given precise instructions on how her grandsons
were to be received in foreign ports. They were to
be granted no royal honours whatsoever. The Prince
of Wales's argument that they should at least be
accorded such honours as were meted out to other
foreign princes cut no ice with the Queen. Self-pride,
she maintained, was something to be discouraged in
princes. In practice, the matter was left to the captain
of the *Bacchante*. Sensibly, while not advertising the
presence of the princes on his ship, he never prevented courtesies being paid by any foreign rulers who
wished to do so.

Therefore, on their arrival at the Cape (which
could hardly be called foreign) Eddy and George
were given no official reception. Indeed, with the
Colony in a state of war, this was hardly the time for
jollification. Their advent went all but unremarked
(even the newspapers remained astonishingly mute)
and it was not until the *Bacchante* had been in Simon's
Bay for five days that the two princes visited Cape
Town. They were to spend ten days as the guests of
the new Governor, Sir Hercules Robinson.

*The Detached Squadron, lying at anchor off Simonstown.
H.M.S. Bacchante is the second last ship on the right.*

Climbing into an open, canopied cart drawn by four white horses, the young princes were rattled along the very road that Prince Alfred had taken twenty years before, beside the sandy shoreline, through the firs and pines and oaks of the suburbs and finally into Cape Town itself. The city had grown considerably since Prince Alfred's first visit. It was altogether more Victorian; its tone more mercantile, its streets more animated, its public buildings more assertive. Yet it was the vestiges of its earlier character that caught the attention of the princes. 'We admired some of the old Dutch mansions;' they wrote (or rather, Mr Dalton wrote for them), 'they are fine and massively built, with heavy dormer windows and little panes, but the roofs are flat. They are chiefly now inhabited by the Malays and other Coloured people that make up the bulk of the population of Cape

Town. The Dutch and Europeans have migrated to the suburbs. . . .

And as an unchanging backdrop to this bustling and richly varied city rose Table Mountain, 'towering up like a black massive wall and covered on its flat top with a white fleecy cloud'.

At four o'clock on that afternoon of 21 February, the party turned into the city's famous oak avenue and alighted at the whitewashed Government House. The princes were met b Sir Hercules and Lady Robinson. The doors of all the rooms in the house, noted the guests without a hint of disapproval, were ornamented with flower paintings, daintily executed by the daughters of the previous governor, the Misses Frere.

For the following ten days Prince Eddy and Prince George were on show. Everyone was anxious to catch a glimpse of them. It was not every day that one could see the future King of England, for that was poor Prince Eddy's status.

Just to look at, Eddy appeared quite normal. Now seventeen years old, he was tall and slender, with his mother's narrow head, if not her marvellous beauty. To those who did not know him well, his lethargy could be mistaken for something else, dignity, calm, even serious-mindedness. 'I think the eldest is better suited to his situation,' noted someone who met him at the time, 'he is shy and not demonstrative, but he does the right things as a gentleman in a quiet way. It is well that he should be more reticent and reflective than the younger boy.'

Reticent Prince Eddy might have been; reflective he certainly was not. But provided Mr Dalton remained firmly at his elbow, and the talk stayed at a fairly banal level, Eddy could get by.

Of the vivacity of the fifteen-year-old Prince George there was no doubt. Much shorter than his brother, he was an attractive, snubnosed ('your impudent snout', his doting mother called his nose), bright-eyed boy. But whereas Eddy's quiet manner sprang from a lack of personality, George's ebullience masked a considerable strength of character. Life in the navy was doing for him exactly what it was meant to be doing for Eddy: it was developing in him a sense of discipline and a sense of duty. These were lessons which Prince George would never unlearn.

The princes' stay at Government House was relatively quiet. For one thing the visit was private; for another, the news from Natal was anything but cheering. 'We have kept as quiet here as we could;' they reported, 'there have been no balls and no entertainments of any sort, for neither the people nor ourselves are at all in the humour for such things.'

But, of course, there was some social activity. The youngsters had to be kept amused and Lady Robinson would have been less than human had she not wanted to take some advantage of the fact that she had two of Queen Victoria's grandsons under her wing. She held one large afternoon reception at which the band of the 91st Regiment played under the trees in the garden. There were several small dinner parties; among the guests was Saul Solomon, owner of the *Cape Argus* and compiler of a lavish book on the visit of Prince Alfred in 1860. There was a visit to a Dutch Reformed Church bazaar, a climb up Table Mountain, a garden party given by the Van der Byls ('driving there by Rondebosch, the lanes are just like these in England, the same trees and hedges') and, less romantically, a visit to the lunatic asylum and leper colony on Robben Island. They went for walks and drives (to Paarl and Stellenbosch on one occasion) and on tours of inspection. 'We passed an ostridge farm,' named Prince George painstakingly in his diary, 'and saw a good many ostridges.'

Cetshwayo

Chis far from eloquent observation was promptly transformed, by the well-meaning Mr Dalton, into a four-page dissertation on the appearance, habits, uses and profitability of ostriches.

One of the most interesting visits was to Cetshwayo, the captive Zulu King. Cetshwayo was being kept on a little farm 'Oude Molen'., a few miles from Care Town. Having dismembered his country after the recent Zulu War, the British were somewhat puzzled as to what should be done with him.

To look at, and to speak to, Cetshwayo was a most impressive figure. Tall, bulky, with enormous thighs and legs – the whole squeezed into unbecoming European dress – Cetshwayo was a man of great dignity. He was delighted to meet the grandsons of the almost mythical Queen Victoria. Speaking through an interpreter with great speed and emphasis, the Zulu King took this opportunity of saying how much he longed to be set free to return to Zululand. Once back among his own people, nothing, he assured the princes, would induce him again to disobey the commands of 'his mother, the Queen of England'

And he was prepared to go further than this. With Britain now at war with the Boers, Cetshwayo was all for helping the British; for 'washing his spears in the blood of the Boers'.

'Let me go,' he entreated the wide-eyed youngsters, 'and I will walk through the Boers, who, you see, after all, are your enemies and not your friends as you supposed . . . let me go, I will do it now.'

Cetshwayo seemed, noted the princes, 'a blood-thirsty old chap'.

Far more interesting, as far as Eddy and Georgie were concerned, than Cetshwayo's politics was Cetshwayo's establishment. In his little house, bare by choice of all furniture, squatted his four moun-tainous wives ('16 & 17 stone . . . very fine women, all over six feet' reported Prince George to his mother) and in a huge iron pot one of his servants was happily brewing 'Kaffir beer'.

From a framed engraving on the wall there gazed down on this sybaritic scene a portrait of Cetshwayo's 'mother' – a no doubt heartily disapproving Queen Victoria.

4

Throughout the princes' stay at Government House, the news from the front had become steadily worse. Defeat followed defeat and then, on the evening of 27 February, Sir Hercules Robinson received a tele-gram to say that the British had suffered a devastating reversal at Majuba Hill, on the Natal-Transvaal bor-der. Their commander, General Sir George Colley, had lost his life during the battle. The Colony was appalled. That the might of imperial Britain should be not only challenged but checked by a handful of ill-trained and ill-equipped Boers seemed scarcely comprehensible. 'This is really a dredful war is it not?' wrote Prince George to his mother. 'All these poor people killed & also General Colley.'

It was in this atmosphere of all-pervading gloom that the princes were obliged to put in their one official appearance. On the morning of 3 March 1881 they received two addresses of welcome at Government House. One was from the local Malay community, the other from the Mayor and his council. A less auspicious moment for representing the all-conquering, all-powerful Queen-Empress could hardly be imagined but, willy-nilly, the young princes had to go through with it. Looking spruce in their dark-blue uniforms and gleaming buttons, and hedged about by the Governor, Mr Dalton and two of His Excellency's secretaries, Prince Eddy and Prince George entered the reception room. The Malay deputation ('their priests and holy men') was picturesque in the extreme: honey-coloured, heavily bearded old men in towering turbans and flowing silk robes. To their address of welcome Prince Eddy read out an answer to the effect that 'the Queen has no more loyal subjects within the wide limits of British rule than the followers of the faith of Islam'. It was a sweeping claim but no doubt served its purpose.

This short exchange over, the princes, followed by the Governor, Mr Dalton and the two secretaries, withdrew. The Malays were ushered out, the Mayor and his council were ushered in, the princes, the Governor, Mr Dalton and the two secretaries returned, the Mayor read out his address of welcome, and Prince Eddy replied. This time (the princes being in the presence of their compatriots rather than of a subject race) Eddy was allowed, in his brief answer, to make mention of 'the sad circumstances which, for the moment, cast a shadow over this land. . . '.

'Cape Town', commented the *Cape Times* the following day, 'may now fairly claim exemption to any charge of neglectfulness respecting the Imperial Princes.'

Their little ambassadorial gesture made, the youngsters returned to their ship two days later. The *Bacchante* by this time had been brought round from Simonstown into Table Bay. Here, with the rest of the company on the Detached Squadron, the princes waited for further orders. It was fondly imagined that Britain was about to embark on a swift and glorious revenge for the defeat of Majuba. A fresh army under the command of Sir Frederick Roberts was known to have set out for the Cape. For day after day, therefore, while the crews were kept out of mischief with regattas and target practice and games of cricket ashore, everyone waited for the war to be resumed.

It never was. Defeated, Britain was anxious to draw in her horns. A truce was arranged and Gladstone's government entered into negotiations with the victorious Boers. On 21 March 1881 peace was signed between Britain and the Transvaal.

'General Roberts arrived today . . . to take command of the British force for restoring order in the

Transvaal,' wrote the disgruntled Mr Dalton on 29 March, 'but he returns by the next mail to England as they have changed their minds since he left home on the 11th and there is to be no more war. . . . Most of the troops brought out at great expense are to return without landing, and this squadron, brought half across the globe, is to be sent away also, for they have no use for it here.'

The outcome of the negotiations was British recognition of the Transvaal's right to self-government. The imperial surge had been checked. Majuba, in fact, had been the last nail in the coffin of Lord Carnarvon's grandiose scheme for a South African Federation.

No wonder poor Mr Dalton despaired of Britain ever being able to sort out the South African muddle. There were just too many races, too many conflicting interests. It could not be governed as a subject state like India; it could not be developed as an all-British country like Australia. 'The problem of governing South Africa to the advantage and satisfaction of the Dutch, the British and the Natives, is perhaps more difficult of solution than any other which British statesmen have had to face,' he sighed. 'Mr Gladstone once said . . . that after having carefully looked into South African difficulties, he had arrived at the conclusion that the case presented a problem of which he, for one, could not see the solution.'

*The tented cart in which the young princes travelled
at the Cape and which they sent as a present to their
mother, Princess (afterwards Queen) Alexandra.*

But one may be sure that no such ponderous thoughts clouded the minds of Prince Eddy and Prince George as the *Bacchante*, to the relief of everyone aboard, finally sailed away from the Cape on 9 April 1881. The signal, flashed from the flagship late one night to say 'Squadron will sail on Saturday for Melbourne,' had been greeted with great cheers.

Prince George, leaving South Africa at the end of the first Anglo-Boer War, was to return, twenty years later towards the end of the second. Now the sun of imperialism was obscured: then it would be all ablaze.

5

No account of the princes' visit to South Africa can be complete without a reference to their sighting of that legendary ghost ship, the *Flying Dutchman.* The often-repeated tale loses some of its relevance when one knows that the ghostly galleon was spotted by the *Bacchante,* not in its customary position off Cape Point – indeed, not off the coast of South Africa at all – but between Melbourne and Sydney, off Australia. Ever, phantom ships, it seems, can be sadly off-course.

One version of the *Flying Dutchman* legend is that a Dutch sea captain named. Van der Decken was condemned, for some or other reason, to sail the treacherous seas around the Cape of Good Hope for all eternity. And whoever glimpsed this strangely glowing vessel was, according to the legend, certain to be struck by disaster.

Down the years the phantom ship has been described by witnesses of varying degrees of reliability but no account can possibly carry more weight than that of the pedantic, punctilious and unimpeachable Mr Dalton; for it was he, of course, and not Prince George who penned the famous passage:

'At 4 a.m. the *Flying Dutchman* crossed our bows,' runs the entry for 11 July 1881. 'A strange red light as of a phantom ship all aglow, in the midst of which light the masts, spars and sails of a brig 200 yards distant stood out in strong relief as she came up on the port bow. The look out man on the forecastle reported her as close on the port bow, where also the officer of the watch from the bridge clearly saw her, as did also the quarterdeck midshipman, who was sent forward at once to the forecastle; but, on arriving there, no vestige nor any sign whatever of any material ship was to be seen either near or right way to the horizon, the night being clear and the sea calm. Thirteen persons altogether saw her, but whether it was *Van Diemen* or the *Flying Dutchman,* or who else, must remain unknown. The *Tommaline* and *Cleopatra,* who were sailing to our starboard bow, flashed to ask whether we had seen the strange red light.'

The customary disaster was not long in following.

'At 10.45 a.m. the ordinary seaman who had this morning reported the *Flying Dutchman* fell from the foretopmast crosstrees and was smashed to atoms.'

But whoever it was who saw the *Flying Dutchman,* it could not have been Prince Eddy, Prince George or Mr Dalton. At four in the morning, they would all have been sound asleep. The Admiralty had received specific instructions to the effect that the princes were not to keep night watch.

6

Within ten years of the end of this cruise on the *Bacchante,* Prince Eddy was dead. Those ten years had been anything but profitable. The young man never outgrew his apathy. Throughout his short life his air remained that of a sleepwalker. Nothing, not a spell at Cambridge, nor a stint in the army, nor a tour of India, could give any shape to his amorphous personality. He lived an utterly worthless existence, indulging in every sort of dissipation (there was even some talk of a *male* brothel) and falling in and out of love like a schoolboy. The only remedy that anyone could suggest was the conventional one: Eddy must marry and settle down. A good, sensible wife was what was needed.

*The Princess of Wales welcoming her sons, on their
return from their cruise on the Bacchante.*

Luckily, there was one to hand. In December
1891, at the age of twenty-seven, Eddy became
engaged to Princess May of Teck. Although Princess
May's father, the Duke of Teck, was a relatively unimportant German princeling, her mother was a British

princess; like Queen Victoria herself, the Duchess of Teck was a grand-daughter of King George III. And May could not have been more suitable. She was a calm, even-tempered and unemotional young woman with a fund of common sense. For one so shy, she was surprisingly self-confident. Princess May, as Queen Victoria put it, was '*very* sensible and well-informed, a *solid girl* which we want. . . '. She was also very good-looking. Her bearing, as befitted a future queen, was dignified.

But just over a month after the engagement had been announced, Prince Eddy fell ill. It was influenza. This quickly developed into pneumonia, and on 14 January 1892 he died. On his coffin, they laid Princess May's wreath of orange blossom.

As far as the future of the British monarchy was concerned, Prince Eddy's death could hardly have been more opportune: his brother – the conscientious, uncomplicated and energetic Prince George – now became heir presumptive. And not only did George inherit poor Eddy's position, he inherited his fiancée. Princess May was too valuable a jewel for the monarchy to let slip through its fingers. After a decent interval George and May became engaged. In July 1893 they were married.

Throughout the following half-dozen or so years, with the British Empire in the noonday of its splendour, George and May moved always in the light that beat so fiercely on the British throne. The death of Queen Victoria in 1901 and the accession of

Prince George's father, as King Edward VII, merely increased the brilliance of their position. One of Prince George's first duties, as heir apparent, was to undertake a world tour. Thus in 1901, at a time of high imperial emotion – for the British Empire was locked in the most significant struggle of its history – George and May, as Duke and Duchess of Cornwall and York, visited embattled South Africa.

PRINCE GEORGE AND
PRINCESS MAY

1

ON THE MORNING OF 13 AUGUST 1901, IN POURING RAIN,
h.m.s. *Ophir* dropped anchor off Durban. Aboard
the luxurious white liner were the Duke and Duchess
of Cornwall and York: Prince George and Princess
May. The royal couple were in the course of a tour that
was to last for eight months, during which they would
have visited Gibraltar, Malta, Port Said, Colombo,
Singapore, Australia, New Zealand, Mauritius, South
Africa and Canada. At the conclusion of the voyage
Prince George in his methodical fashion would note
that they had travelled 45,000 miles (33,000 by sea and
12,000 by land), laid 21 foundation stones, received
544 addresses, presented 4,329 medals and shaken
hands, officially, with 24,855 people. It was, in fact,
the first of those great royal tours that were to become
such a feature of the Empire and Commonwealth in
the century that lay ahead.

H.M.S. *Ophir,* the ship now riding at anchor off Durban, had been especially chartered by the Admiralty from the Orient Line. Double-funnelled, painted a dazzling white and completely refurnished, it was reckoned to be the most sumptuous liner afloat. Its 'drawing-room' was rich in velvet, brocade and leather; its dining-saloon positively baronial in atmosphere ('rather gaudy' was Princess May's tart comment); the royal staterooms were panelled in white and fitted with basins of alabaster and onyx.

All this grandeur was rather wasted on the royal couple, for the Duke, after his years in the navy, always preferred small, unpretentious, cabin-like rooms, while the Duchess loathed travelling by sea, no matter now comfortable the accommodation. 'I *detest* the sea . . .' she admitted on this voyage, 'it is purgatory to me and makes me miserable and depressed.' The trouble was that Princess May suffered from seasickness; a condition that all the panelling and alabaster and onyx in the world could do nothing to alleviate. She had a swing cot rigged up in her cabin, and it was here, misguidedly, that she spent much of the voyage.

The *Ophir* having sailed from Portsmouth on 16 March 1901 (all of them – King Edward VII, Queen Alexandra, Prince George and Princess May – had sobbed unrestrainedly on parting), it was over halfway through its long voyage by the time it reached South Africa from Australia in mid-August.

As the sand bar across the narrow mouth of Durban's lovely bay prevented the entry of large shipping, the royal party was obliged to trans-ship from their great white liner to the tug *Panther*. The sea, in spite of the rain, was calm, and this spared Their Royal Highnesses the indignity of being swung overboard and onto the *Panther* in basket seats. The firing of two rockets signalled the crossing of the bar and, at just before half past eleven, Prince George and Princess May stepped ashore in Natal. They were greeted by the Governor, Sir Henry McCallum, and, despite the drizzle, a wildly cheering crowd of some 40,000 people.

The Duke and Duchess of York made an extremely attractive couple Now thirty-six, Prince George was slender, erect and sun-tanned, his beard neatly trimmed, his moustache brushed up, his eyes a bright and candid blue. He wore, for this occasion, the dark-blue uniform of an Admiral of the Fleet. Across his coat slanted the broad ribbon of the Garter, his chest glittered with decorations, on his head was a gold-laced cocked hat.

In the twenty years since his last visit to South Africa, Prince George's character had crystal-lised. Although he was always to retain a certain blustery cheerfulness, Prince George had lost his boyish impishness. He was by now the seri-ous, straightforward and integrated personality that he was to remain throughout his life. He might not have been a clever man, but he was a consistent and conscientious one. This tour, moreover, was giving Prince George an increased self-confidence. Away from the somewhat over-powering presence of his father, King Edward VII, and obliged to play the central role at every function, Prince George was gaining assurance by the day. All in all, as the heir apparent and future King George V, Prince George was acquitting himself admirably.

The same was true of Princess May, the future Queen Mary. If the crowds thronging the dockside at Durban had been prepared for the Duke's bluff good looks, the Duchess's beauty came as a surprise. The thirty-three-year-old Princess May photographed badly and her reserve tended to give her a somewhat stolid look. But when she relaxed and particularly when she smiled, the effect could be radiant. She had great charm of manner, great dignity and wore her clothes with great authority.

Unfortunately, her clothes were not much help to her on this tour for the court was still in mourning for Queen Victoria, who had died earlier that year. Thus, except at sea, when grey and white were permissible, Princess May was obliged to wear black. But whether in mourning or not, many of the features of an appearance that was tu remain almost unchanged for the next half-century were already there: the towering toques, the elaborately dressed hair, the high collars, the sumptuous fabrics, he fur trimmings, the parasols and the upright, rigidly corseted bearing.

Already, Princess May could never be mistaken for anything other than royal.

The tour was having its effect on the Duchess's personality no less than on that of her husband. Extremely shy by nature, Princess May was always more so at the brilliant and frivolous Edwardian court. In the company of the ebullient King Edward VII, the vivacious Queen Alexandra and their light-hearted circle, Princess may felt gauche, stiff, tongue-tied. She was too serious, too intelligent, too withdrawn. Nor was she reckoned to be quite royal enough for her position. Her father, the Duke of Teck, had been the son of a morganatic marriage; his was a flaw in her ancestry that some at court were not prepared to forget. Their attitude tended to make her even more reserved.

But now, when she was being forced make an effort, to hold always the centre of the stage, Princess May was proving that she was quite capable of doing so. 'Her Royal Highness has quite got over her shyness abroad, and almost enjoys a procession,' reported one of her ladies. 'Her smile is commented on in every paper and her charm of manner; in fact she is having a *succès fou!*'

'She is at last coming out of her shell,' she wrote later, 'and will electrify them at home as she has everyone here.'

The reasons for this emergence of Princess May were twofold: she was a passionate sightseer, deeply interested in all the strange, new places that she was visiting; and she shared her husband's strong sense of royal obligation. The British monarchy, to her, was a sacrosanct institution; therefore, to add to its lustre Princess May was prepared to bring her own considerable capacities into full play. Although she could not entirely conquer her shyness (South African observers would occasionally refer to her 'rare smiles' and her 'slight unapproachability') her sense of vocation during this tour could not be faulted.

Indeed, for the first time in her career one gets a glimpse of that extraordinary effort of will that was to turn the retiring Princess May into the magnificent Queen Mary.

2

Ignoring the drizzle, which had reduced the decorations to a streaked and pulpy mess, the Duke and Duchess greeted the assembled dignitaries on the dock and drove into the city of Durban. The city's much-vaunted civic progress – its electricity, its trams, its pillared and pedimented Town Hall, its red-brick railway station, its inevitable statue of Queen Victoria – could not obliterate its more exotic atmosphere. Durban at the turn of the century was one of the most colourful cities in the Empire, its vegetation as lush as ever, the already kaleidoscopic mixture of its population further enriched by the importation and subsequent proliferation of the Indian community. In fact, as the royal couple stood on the specially erected (and mercifully canopied) dais in the Royal Albert Park, they were able to come to some appreciation of this *mélange* of races. Seldom, if ever, could Prince George have received addresses of welcome from so many differing communities.

From Albert Park they drove through the crowded streets to a luncheon given by the Mayor, Ernest Acutt. The mourning for Queen Victoria had meant a cutting down of certain functions; a line had to be drawn, it seems, between what was considered duty and what mere merry-making. There were to be no state dinners or balls, but civic luncheons were allowed. With an easy conscience, therefore, the royal party sat themselves down at the Mayor's table.

*Stiffly, the royal party poses at Government House, Pietermaritzburg.
Prince George (in busby) stands in the centre. Princess
May is seated to his right, Lord Kitchener to his left.*

*Mayor Ernest Acute presenting an address of welcome to Prince
George and Princess May in Albert Park, Durban. The white
chairs behind the royal couple were again to be used, almost half
a century later, for the state visit of their son, King George VI.*

The meal over, Their Royal Highnesses left by train for Pietermaritzburg, the capital of the Colony. Here they were to spend two nights at Government House. They left behind them in Durban, noted one breathless reporter, a legacy of love and loyalty such as the city had not experienced since the visit of Prince George's uncle, Prince Alfred.

They also left the rain. Their stay in Pietermaritzburg was marked by brilliant sunshine. The elegant little city (neatly planned by the Boers in the days when they had fondly imagined that it was to be *their* capital) was unquestionably British in character. It was a conglomeration of red-brick, cast-iron-verandahed villas and pompously proportioned public buildings. Here the royal couple carried out a strenuous programme. Prince George unlocked the door of the newly completed Town Hall with a golden key (in his speech he mentioned the fact that the foundation stone of the previous building had been laid by Prince Alfred); he reviewed troops in the park (Lord Kitchener was there and the Prince reported to his father that the famous soldier was 'looking remarkably fit and well and he has grown fat'); he received a party of Zulu warriors, whose customary and bloodcurdling war-dance was forbid-den, apparently because war-dancing fell under the heading of merry-making. When one of the Zulu spokesmen bemoaned the death of Queen Victoria, claiming that 'the sun had set and deep darkness was over the land', Prince George was quick to assure him that, with the reign of Edward VII, the sun had risen again. On the last evening in the capital, the royal party presided over an evening reception, followed by an investiture.

Princess May, looking always so elegant, if sombre, in black, performed no duties of her own other than to receive, from a deputation of admiring ladies, a memento of the visit. It was a table gong, made unexpectedly of three – presumably exploded – 'pom-pom' shells, all mounted on rhinoceros horn.

On the morning of 15 August the Duke and Duchess took the train back to Durban and later that day, watched by a tremendous crowd, boarded the tug that was to carry them across the bar to the *Ophir,* lying white and glittering in the open and now sunlit sea. They sailed, that afternoon, for Cape Town.

3

The shadow lying across the royal visit of 1901 was, of course, the Anglo-Boer War. For almost two years the two Boer republics, the Transvaal and the Orange Free State, had been challenging (and at one stage almost crippling) the might of the British Empire.

The reasons for the war were manifold and complicated, but in the main it had come as a result of yet another British attempt to bring all the peoples and territories of South Africa under her control. The tentative federal schemes of men like Sir George Grey and Lord Carnarvón had been succeeded by the far more aggressive ambitions of men like Cecil

Rhodes and Sir Alfred Milner. The sun, at this high
noon of British imperialism, shone hottest in South
Africa; there was just no place, in this imperial noonday, for these two hostile, independent and unsophisticated Boer republics. When they continued to resist
imperial pressure, war became inevitable. But few
had imagined that they would put up so prolonged
and spirited a fight. Those who assumed that the fall
of the Transvaal capital, Pretoria, to Lord Roberts in
June 1900 would mean an end to the war, had been
proved wrong. The Boers, to the chagrin, bafflement
and embarrassment of the British, had continued
to fight, skilfully, stubbornly and with a maddening
inability to know when they were beaten.

Yet they could surely not last much longer. Lord
Kitchener assured Prince George that the end was
in sight. 'He wished me to tell you', reported the
Prince from Natal to King Edward VII, 'that everybody from himself downwards is working hard to finish the war. . . . He seemed very hopeful, especially
having accounted for 839 Boers last week; he does
not believe that there are more than 14,000 left in
the field and they must be precious short of horses.'

Prince George was only too aware of many of the
lessons of the war against the Boers. He mentioned
it in every speech, he discussed it at every gathering.
He, like so many of his countrymen, had been deeply
disturbed by the early successes of the Boers, by the
tremendous effort needed to subdue them, and by the
violently anti-British feeling in Europe. As far as he

was concerned, the one encouraging factor to emerge from this prolonged and humiliating struggle was the support given to the mother country by her sons in the Empire. On a wave of – often unthinking – emotion, colonial Englishmen in Canada, Australia, New Zealand and, of course, the Cape and Natal, came to the aid of Britain. It was, in truth, as a gesture of appreciation to these colonies that Prince George and Princess May were undertaking this tour. This was to be the monarchy's thanks for 'the loyalty and devotion which have prompted the spontaneous aid so liberally offered by all the colonies in the South African War, and the splendid gallantry of (the) Colonial troops'.

There had, at one stage, been some doubt as to the advisability of the royal couple visiting the country to which all this aid was being so unstintingly rushed. After all, the war was by no means over, and even the city of Pietermaritzburg had once been too close to the front for complete comfort. But at the urgings of that arch-imperialist, the British Colonial Secretary, Joseph Chamberlain, and of the no-less-jingoistic High Commissioner in South Africa, Sir Alfred Milner, South Africa was included. The royal visit, reckoned Chamberlain, would 'have a very good political effect and would encourage the loyal party in South Africa, while its abandonment would be regarded as a triumph by the Boer press in the Colony and its supporters'.

Nowhere was that 'loyal party' in South Africa more loyal than in the Colony of Natal, and in

Pietermaritzburg Prince George gave thanks for this. 'Never in our history', he said, 'did the pulse of Empire beat more in unison, and the blood which has been shed on the veld has sealed for ever our unity, based upon a common loyalty and determination to share, each according to our strength, the common burden.'

These, of course, were the sentiments of the day. Prince George, as a simple man and an unquestioning imperialist, was merely putting into words the thoughts of the majority of his kinsmen, in Britain and the colonies. It was left to a more farseeing and enlightened personality, James Rose Innes, the Attorney-General of the Cape, to give voice to the deeper lessons of the war.

James Rose Innes was one of the leading figures of a small body of moderates uncomfortably pitted against the jingoism of people like Rhodes, Milner and Kitchener. He adhered to what was known as the Cape liberal tradition: a lonely and unpopular path to tread at a time of political extremism (on the part of both Briton and Boer) and one which led him to the position where he was accused of being pro-Boer. Innes was nothing of the sort. It was simply that he was afraid that the excesses of the British military authorities would leave a legacy of hatred in their wake. He had the good sense to realise that, once the war was over, Briton and Boer would have to learn to live together. His was the voice of liberalism, always too little heard in South Africa.

Taking advantage of the atmosphere of high emotion engendered by the visit of the heir to the British throne, James Rose Innes delivered an important speech. On the eve of Prince George's arrival in Cape Town, he addressed a luncheon for some three hundred political delegates from all over the Cape Colony. Once the war was over, he declared, no vindictiveness must be shown towards the enemy. The victors must be magnanimous and the past forgotten. Boer and Briton must work together for the future good of South Africa.

4

If one thing characterised the decorations in Cape Town more than another, it was the triumphal arch. Nothing, not the bunting nor the flags nor the banners nor the potted palms nor the great swags of greenery, could match the arches. They were everywhere; each one more grandiose than the last. Crenellated, turreted, columned, domed, they spanned every principal thoroughfare in the city. There was a medieval arch on the Grand Parade, there was a Byzantine arch in Greenmarket Square, there was a classical arch at the entrance to Government Avenue (designed as the forerunner of a permanent structure to be erected later), there was a massive battlemented arch of mock stone astride the railway line at Woodstock station. If the visit of the heir to the throne turned out to be anything less than triumphant, it would not be for want of appropriate arches.

The visit opened, however, on a somewhat muted note. H.M.S. *Ophir* arrived in Simon's Bay on 18 August 1901, which happened unfortunately to be a Sunday. So the day was spent quietly. In the afternoon the royal couple landed without ceremony and spent a few hours at Admiralty House. They returned to the *Ophir* later that afternoon.

On Monday morning things began in earnest. It was, reported one of the welcoming party, 'a *lovely* morning, and the sea looked its best'. At half past ten the Governor, Sir Walter Hely-Hutchinson, with his lady and a host of dignitaries, ministers and officials welcomed the Duke and Duchess at a specially erected landing-stage at the Simonstown docks. 'It was all so simple and natural that really one felt quite at ease,' reported James Rose Innes to his wife. A party of sailors dragged the royal carriage down the hill to Simonstown station and once a group of schoolchildren had sung 'God Save lhe King' ('very much out of tune', reports Innes), the train carried the distinguished company on to Cape Town Here they alighted at a special platform, resplendent in cream and gold, and the royal couple were led to what can only be described as a pagoda on the Grand Parade. Once the customary addresses of welcome had been presented, the Duke and Duchess drove through the lavishly decorated and wildly acclaiming streets to Government House.

Triumphal arch in Sir Lowry Road, Cape Town.

Some of the African chiefs who came to pay homage in Cape Town.

To Prince George, the growth of Cape Town during the two decades since his last visit was very apparent. 'Apart from their tasteful decoration,' he said in a speech later that day, 'the principal streets through which we have passed offer an aspect very different from that which they possessed twenty years ago.' They did indeed. Cape Town, by the year 1901, was not only an extremely beautiful city, but a vital and expanding one. Its setting, between the sea and Table Mountain, remained superb and its public buildings boasted the supreme self-confidence and uninhibited variety of all high-Victorian architecture. 'Fundamentally,' as one journal put it, 'the old Dutch features have been superseded by others of more modern and British character.' And, to this chief seaport of an extremely wealthy hinterland, the war had brought an added importance. No colonial capital, at the turn of the century, occupied a more important position clear Cape Town.

The royal couple spent five days in Cape Town. During that time, they were on constant show. When Queen Alexandra wrote to say that they must 'rest more', Prince George answered that is 'is all very well for you and Papa to say we mustn't do so much but it is impossible to help it. Our stay in each place is so short, that everything has to be crammed into it.'

Everything was certainly crammed into the Cape Town visit. There was a levee in the Throne Room of the recently built Houses of Parliament; African chiefs came to pay homage and to lay their gifts of animal skins on the lawns of Government House; in sparkling

sunshine the royal party drove out to Groote Schuur, ⎭
the famous home of Cecil John Rhodes (Rhodes
himself was away in England) and had luncheon in
its Cape Dutch styled rooms; Prince George was cer-
emonially installed as Chancellor of the University of
Cape Town; at Government House, the Duke held
an investiture (James Rose Innes was knighted: 'I was
kept bobbing all the evening like a marionette,' he
told his wife); the buttress stone was laid for the new
St George's Cathedral; there were garden parties and
evening receptions and breathtaking firework displays.

One discordant note only was struck during the
course of this five-day-long jamboree. The *Vierkleur,*
the flag of the Transvaal, was defiantly hoisted from
the offices of *Ons Land,* the Afrikaner newspaper. A
party of Australian troopers, incensed by what they
considered to be an open insult to the royal visitors,
promptly ripped the flag down and burned it.

Throughout this strenuous round of activity, Prince George was supported by Princess May.
'Darling May is of the greatest possible help to me
and works very hard,' reported the Duke to Queen
Alexandra. 'I don't think I could have done all this
without her.' Her one solo duty – the laying of the
foundation stone for the Victoria Nurses' Home at
the Somerset Hospital – Princess May carried out
with great charm and dignity. She received, of course,
the customary presents: among them a vast fan of
black ostrich feathers with a diamond-encrusted handle; an ivory paper-knife bearing the badge of the

'Loyal Women's Guild of South Africa', set with diamonds, rubies and sapphires; and, from the De Beers
Company, no fewer than 600 diamonds. To Princess
May, who adored jewellery and would always wear
it to such spectacular effect, this must have been a
highly appreciated gift.

Prince George and Princess May had had to leave
their four little children, whose ages ranged from
seven to one years, in the care of King Edward VII
and Queen Alexandra. Quite naturally, the youngsters were often in their mother's thoughts. A woman
guest at a reception at Government House was
touched to be told by the normally reserved Duchess
that she had that day received a letter from her eldest son Edward (known to his parents as David; afterwards King Edward VIII and then Duke of Windsor);
it was the first that he had ever written in ink.

One result of this royal tour was to deepen Prince
George's love and admiration for his wife. Both rather
inarticulate and undemonstrative people', George
and May – even after eight years of marriage – found
it difficult to express their intimate feelings towards
each other. Thus it was in a letter, written when the
tour was over, that the husband revealed his sentiments to his wife.

'Somehow I can't tell you, so I take the first opportunity of writing to say how deeply I am indebted to
you darling for the splendid way in which you supported and helped me during our long Tour; it was
you who made it a success. . . . If you had not come

with me, it would not have been at all a success. . .
. Although I have often told it you before, I repeat
it once more, that I love you darling child, with my
whole heart and soul and thank God every day that I
have such a wife as you, who is such a great help and
support to me and I believe loves me too.'

5

On Friday 23 August 1901 Prince George and Princess
May sailed away from South Africa. They were bound
for Canada, where they were to spend several weeks. Not
until 1 November 1901 did they again reach England.

This great royal tour was to have a profound effect
on Prince George and on his conception of the role
of the monarchy in relation to the Empire. The voyage had been undertaken at a time when tremendous change was taking place in the structure of the
Empire. Whereas both the Prince's grandmother,
Queen Victoria, and his father, Edward VII, reigned
over a collection of British dependencies, of colonies
of British people who looked to England as home,
Prince George, as King George V, would one day reign
over a commonwealth of separate nations. Slowly a
British family of independent states was evolving, states
with a dual loyalty – first to their own nation, and then
to the mother country. No longer were these simply
Englishmen living abroad; they were beginning to
think of themselves as Australians or New Zealanders
or Canadians or South Africans – different from
Englishmen, and different from each other.

*Arriving home after an absence of eight months, Prince George
and Princess May exchange their first words with their eldest son,
David (afterwards King Edward VIII and Duke of Windsor).
Behind the boy stand King Edward VII and Queen Alexandra.*

And the symbolic link between these rapidly
expanding nations and the country from which they
had sprung was the Crown. The people of Australia
or New Zealand or Canada or the South African
colonies knew little and cared increasingly less about

British party politics. As Prince George had seen for himself, colonial governments managed their own affairs; men born in the colonies ran their own countries. What these diverse people cared about was the imperial ideal, embodied in the person of the monarch. Not only did trade, defence and shared traditions bind these increasingly self-sufficient countries to Britain; more important was their joint allegiance to a common sovereign.

And this great journey of the heir to the throne, at a time when royal tours were a rarity, seemed to crystallise this still-fluid situation, to prove that the Crown was indeed the bond that linked these countries, not only to Britain but to each other.

In South Africa the position was infinitely more complicated. There was no such thing as a South African nation; not by a long chalk. Only in the Cape and Natal (as yet un-united) did a section of the European population feel this loyalty towards the Crown. The majority of Afrikaners living in the Cape Colony felt no such pull. The Transvaal Boers owed their allegiance to the Transvaal and the Free State Boers owed theirs to the Orange Free State. The various African nations, their power broken, might swear fealty to the Great White Queen and fling their animal skins at the feet of her grandson, but their first loyalty went, quite naturally, to their own tribes. And what of the Malays and the Coloured people and the Indians?

It was to be the task of the peacemakers to mould not only the soon-to-be-vanquished Boers but this entire hotch-potch of peoples in the sub-continent, into a single nation; a nation, moreover, that would be ready to give its allegiance to the British monarchy.

Princess Christian

1

ON A BRILLIANTLY MOONLIT NIGHT, EARLY IN SEPTEMBER 1904, an attempt was made to steal a body from its grave in Pretoria cemetery. The surface earth was dug up but the stone slab covering the coffin proved too heavy to lift, and the attempt was temporarily abandoned. Embarrassed, the authorities decided to hush up the incident. The grave was hurriedly filled in and no guard set over it.

A few nights later a second attempt was made. With picks and shovels stolen from the sexton's store-house, the earth was again removed and the stone slab laid bare. But as the thieves were about to prise up the slab, they were disturbed and had to flee. This time there was no playing down of the affair. The grave was once more filled in and a special police guard set up.

The grave was that of Queen Victoria's grand-son, Prince Christian Victor of Schleswig-Holstein. Christian Victor was the eldest son of Queen Victoria's third daughter, Helena. Despite his uncompromisingly Germanic title, Prince Christian Victor was very much a British prince. His father – Prince Christian of Schleswig-Holstein – had been allowed to marry the Queen's daughter Helena on one condition only: the husband must be prepared to live in the wife's country, England. The marriages of Queen Victoria's two elder daughters to foreign princes had led to nothing but trouble; those recurrent Continental wars were always finding members of the Queen's family on opposing sides. Moreover, as Queen Victoria grew older, so did she become more anxious to keep her remaining daughters close to her side. To ensure this, she insisted that they marry tame, politically uncommitted husbands, who were ready to make their homes in England.

Prince Christian of Schleswig-Holstein was just such a prince. Obligingly he married Princess Helena ('I consider the matter as settled,' announced Queen Victoria after one meeting with Prince Christian) and knuckled down to life in the shadow of his formidable mother-in-law.

It was quite natural, therefore, that their eldest son, Prince Christian Victor, born in 1867, should be raised as a British prince. Wellington College was followed by Oxford, and Oxford by Sandhurst. The Prince then played his part in those various *fin de siècle* campaigns by which imperial Britain maintained her sway over the recalcitrant natives: in India, in West Africa, and in the

Sudan. With his rapidly balding head, his almost imperceptible moustache and his somewhat vapid blue eyes, Prince Christian Victor (or Christle as his family called him) might not have looked particularly dynamic but he managed to pick up the odd decoration here and the odd mention in dispatches there. In October 1899, at the outbreak of the Anglo-Boer War, he joined the staff of Lord Roberts and set out for South Africa. He was then thirty-two years of age. 'I hope and pray', wrote the old Queen in her diary for 1 January 1900, 'dear Christie will be spared. . . .'

He was not. By the end of October 1900 dear Christle was dead. It was not, alas, on the field of glory that Prince Christian Victor met his end. His death, like his life, lacked drama. He died, after a fortnight's illness, of enteric fever in the Yeomanry Hospital in Pretoria. His family always maintained that he had contracted the fever by drinking iced water after a strenuous game of tennis.

Arrangements to ship his body back to England were stopped by a telegram from the Queen. He was to be buried in Pretoria. Before leaving home, Christian Victor had apparently expressed the wish that, in the event of his death, he was to be laid among his comrades. Thus on 1 November 1900 he was buried in the Pretoria cemetery. In time, his grave was marked by a cross of granite from the Balmoral estate and surrounded by a low cast-iron railing.

There it lay, undisturbed, for four years until that week in September 1904, when two attempts were made to steal the coffin. The police believed, or said they believed, that it had been the work of 'three Australians'. The men ('sweepings of the streets of Australian cities' as one journal put it) had hatched a plot whereby they would steal the coffin, spirit it away to the Zoutpansberg mountains, and later, while on a simulated hunting expedition, would pretend to have stumbled across it. They would then claim a reward for having discovered it.

Or there could have been a quite different motive. Paul Kruger, the President of the South African Republic – the Transvaal – had died, in exile in Switzerland, in July that year. By September 1904 arrangements were already in hand for the bringing back of his body for burial in the Pretoria cemetery. Could resentment against the British, in the minds of two or three Boers, have been such that they did not want the body of their beloved President to lie beside that of the grandson of the hated British sovereign?

Giving weight to both theories was the fact that the grave of Prince Christian Victor was about to have the spotlight of public interest focused on it. For the late Prince's mother, Princess Helena (or Princess Christian as she was popularly known) was to pay a pilgrimage to her son's grave. Those 'three Australians' might well have imagined that a reward would be offered to whoever discovered the coffin;

the authorities would surely go to any lengths to ensure that the mourning mother was not faced by an empty tomb. And, on the other hand, might the empty grave of Queen Victoria's grandson beside the newly filled grave of the great Boer leader not seem like just retribution for Afrikanerdom's defeat at the hands of the British? In the bitter aftermath of the Anglo-Boer War, when the Governor of the Transvaal, Lord Milner, was busily trying to stamp out even the Afrikaner's language, such a thing was not inconceivable.

The grave of Queen Victoria's grandson, Prince Christian Victor, in the Pretoria cemetery, with an inset photograph of the Prince.

2

In the year 1904, Princess Christian turned fifty-eight. She had always been the least known of Queen Victoria's five daughters: less brill ant than the eldest Vicky, the German Empress; less serious-minded than Alice, Grand Duchess of Hesse; less artistic than Louise, Duchess of Argyll; less closely associated with her mother than Beatrice, Princess of Battenberg. Princess Christian's life had been relatively uneventful, devoted to the care of her husband and their five children, and to the royal round of foundation-stone laying, bazaar opening and hospital visiting.

Yet Princess Christian was more than a royal cipher. Her apparently negative characteristics had their own strengths: she was a skilled conciliator, a painstaking organiser, a practical benefactress. Her celebrated good works had everything to do with benevolence and nothing to do with show. Behind that grand, authoritarian façade beat a sympathetic heart. If Princess Christian had not inherited her mother's shrewdness, she had something of her more sensible, honest-to-goodness qualities.

She also had her figure. At middle age Princess Christian was short, tubby and far from chic. Her hats might be a-flutter with ostrich feathers and her figure rigidly corseted but Princess Christian always looked exactly what she was: a high-born lady with a talent for organisation and a warm heart.

Not until two years after the end of the Anglo-Boer War was Princess Christian able to pay a visit to the country in which her eldest son lay buried. On 20 August 1904 she sailed from Southampton in the *Walmer Castle*. (The sailing date had been altered to allow for a suitable refurnishing of the royal accommodation.) Travelling with Princess Christian was her eldest daughter, the thirty-four-year-old Princess Victoria. With her fringed and frizzled hair, her tiny waist and her feather boas, Victoria looked like a pale carbon copy of that *beau ideal* of all turn-of-the-century princesses – Queen Alexandra.

The admiration was not reciprocated. Alexandra always referred to the long-nosed Victoria as 'The Snipe'.

There had once been some talk of Princess Victoria marrying either Prince Eddy or Prince George (this was in the days before Princess May was being seriously considered) but Alexandra had refused to hear of it. 'So the Xtians have been following you about with their lovely Snipe!' wrote Alexandra to her son George. 'Well, it *will* be a pleasure to welcome that beauty as your bride. . . .'

But neither Alexandra nor anyone else welcomed Victoria as a bride, and in 1904, when she accompanied her mother to South Africa, she was still unmarried.

On 6 September, after a seventeen-day voyage, the *Walmer Castle* docked in Table Bay. 'Though the journey will be, as far as possible, a private one,' wrote one South African journalist, 'it cannot fail to excite keen interest among all classes of the King's South African subjects.'

Excite keen interest it certainly did. Any idea of Princess Christian's journey being a private one was swept aside from the moment of her landing. There was a guard of honour, a host of dignitaries, a procession of carriages, an escort of lancers, a colourfully decorated route and wave upon wave of thunderous cheers. And it was the same wherever she went. The royal ladies travelled through South Africa in an atmosphere of extraordinary enthusiasm. Princess Christian had come out on a private pilgrimage to her son's grave; she was everywhere received as King Edward VII's sister, an ambassador of the British Crown.

Princess Christian driving past the Supreme Court, Cape Town, on her way to the station to start her journey through South Africa.

And she was being cast in an even more significant role than this. Could not this British princess – so well known for her benevolence of heart – come to symbolise the start of a new era of peace in South Africa; an end to the bitterness between Boer and Briton? It was noticed that members of the political opposition were invited to the official dinner at Government House. In no time this far from exceptional move was being hailed as a gesture of deep significance. The sinking of political differences in the interests of a common loyalty and kindly sympathy affords an object lesson which should not be lost on others of a much less exalted station in South Africa,' lectured one newspaper. 'If the visit of the Princess does nothing else, it bids fair to draw closer together those bonds of sympathy, sanctified by a community of sorrow and suffering, which should make the South Africa of the future strong and united.'

What the reactions of the plump, autocratic and matter-of-fact Princess Christian were, on being saddled with the duties of an Angel of Peace, one does not know. She was probably happily unaware of it.

3

As far as royal visitors were concerned, Princess Christian was breaking new ground. Hitherto, with the exception of Prince Alfred's visit to the Orange Free State, official royal visits had been confined to the coastal areas; now, in their *train de luxe* (they were making use of Lord Milner's special carriage) Princess

Christian and her daughter travelled through the vast, open, sunbaked heartland of South Africa. With the war over and the peace signed, there was no area of Southern Africa in which they would not be on British-controlled soil.

They planned to go first, via Kimberley, Mafeking and Bulawayo, to the Victoria Falls. They would then return, through Bulawayo and Mafeking, and make for Johannesburg and Pretoria, where Princess Christian would visit her son's grave. Down they would travel into Natal, to Pietermaritzburg and Durban, before returning, via Bloemfontein in the Orange Free State, to the Cape. That they would be able to accomplish this four-thousand-mile journey entirely by train was an indication of the way Southern Africa had progressed in less than two decades.

Fortunately, Princess Victoria was an enthusiastic photographer. There were thus reflected, for the first time in a royal lens, an assortment of backgrounds very different from the usual billowing trees and trim lawns of the royal domains at home. Into the oval and square and oblong windows of the royal photograph albums would be slipped pictures of straggly Government House gardens, dusty battlefields, forlorn railway sidings and the flat, featureless and apparently limitless veld.

Leaving the lushness of the Western Cape, the princesses travelled north-east across the arid Karroo. Their first stop was Kimberley. The discovery of diamonds in the late 1860s had given birth to this close-packed and bustling little centre, quite unlike any other in South Africa. By 1904 the old tented and corrugated-iron shanty town had been transformed into a no less higgledy-piggledy but considerably more substantial-looking city. Its maze of narrow streets boasted two-and even three-storied shops, all rich in cast-iron decoration, and on its fringes lay sprawling red-brick villas in relatively shady gardens.

It was in the most imposing of these brick buildings, the Sanatorium (known later as the Hotel Belgrave), that Princess Christian and her daughter were accommodated for their two-day stay. Their time was given over to the customary royal carousel: the inspection of a mine hospital, a visit to a model village for the employees of the De Beers Mining Company, a tour of a diamond mine (where Princess Christian was given 'seven beautiful diamonds'), a dinner party and the opening of a new children's ward in the Kimberley hospital. (Many years later Princess Christian's second daughter, Princess Marie Louise, visited a local hospital and is said to have astonished the staff by the aplomb with which she downed a considerable quantity of sherry.)

From Kimberley the *train de luxe* went chugging on through hardly less desolate country to Rhodesia. Founded less than fifteen years before, Rhodesia – as far as the white men were concerned – was still a sparsely settled country. Bulawayo, where the royal travellers made their first stop, was hardly more than a village. Their stay here was very brief. The princesses merely left their train long enough to drive through the exceptionally wide streets, to be presented with the obligatory address of welcome (this one was handed over in the shade of a bandstand) and to visit Government House. While Princess Christian was admiring the view from the house, Princess Victoria was clicking away industriously with her camera. Within a couple of hours they returned to their train.

The next stop was the Victoria Falls. For the first time a member of Queen Victoria's family set eyes on that thunderous and spectacular fall of water which had been named in her honour. To mark the occasion, one of the many little islands in the Zambezi was named after Princess Christian. The gesture was to have a touching sequel. Over forty years later, when the Princess's grand-nephew, King George VI, visited the Victoria Falls, he arranged that two other islands be given the names of Princess Christian's daughters: Helena Victoria and Marie Louise. This would complete, cabled King George VI to his by now aged second cousins, 'a little family party at the Victoria Falls'.

On the following day the indefatigable travellers returned south to Bulawayo. From here they visited 'View of the World', the dramatic site in the Matopo Hills where the body of the great Cecil John Rhodes lay buried. Also to the Matopos, to pay homage to the daughter of Queen Victoria, came the chiefs of yet another of those African tribes to have been broken by the encroaching white men – the Matabele. The homage received, Princess Christian returned to Bulawayo and set out almost immediately for the Transvaal.

The royal visit to Rhodesia, trumpeted one leader writer, 'would give Rhodesians a yet keener realisation of the fact that, while doing their good work of expansion and development on the edge of the Empire, they share fully, not only in the glorious heritage of the race, but in all Imperial efforts for the present and aspirations for the future'.

4

Princess Christian spent five days – from 22 to 26 September – in Pretoria. This capital of the recently conquered South African republic, now all a-flutter with Union Jacks, was a surprisingly elegant little city. Indeed, Church Square had an almost Parisian look about it. But with that all resemblance to Paris ended. Pretoria was a stolid, tranquil, unsophisticated city, still very much the capital of a parochial and pastoral people. It remained the heart of Afrikanerdom.

By now, however, there were enough citizens with British sympathies to ensure that Princess Christian and her daughter were given what one newspaper described as an 'adequate' welcome. The weather might have been hot and the streets dusty but the crowd was gratifyingly enthusiastic.

The Princess put one day – Friday 23 September – aside for visiting her son's grave. At first, the news of the desecration had been kept from her but by the time she reached Pretoria she knew all about it. 'Was it not a brutal thing to do?' was her comment on the affair.

For the rest, Princess Christian's stay took on an official character. She laid the foundation stone of an old-age home, she opened a bazaar in the Zoological Gardens and she opened the Princess Christian Park. At an official luncheon she met General Louis Botha, one of the few Boer leaders who was showing a willingness to work together with the British victors towards the creation of a new South African state. In many ways Botha was fast becoming the darling of moderate white opinion, and observers were quick to point to the significance of this meeting between the British princess and the Boer general. Both conciliators by nature, both plump as pouter pigeons, Princess Christian and General Louis Botha seemed to symbolise a coming era of harmony and prosperity.

The other Boer general who would one day become a champion of the imperial connection – Jan Christiaan Smuts – was as yet unprepared for any such hobnobbing with the conquerors. He refused to meet Princess Christian. He and his wife were still too bitter about the outcome of the war. Many years later, when Smuts me. Princess Christian's second daughter, Princess Marie Louise, he admitted to a 'lasting regret that I refused to meet your mother when she made her pilgrimage to see her son's grave'.

In flowered hat and feather boa, Princess Christian sits between her daughter ('The Snipe') and Sir Henry McCallum, Governor of Natal, at Government House, Pietermaritzburg.

Never again would Smuts her slip an opportunity of getting to know a member of a royal family.

That symbol of jingoism, Lord Milner, was Princess Christian's host during the next stage of her journey, her three-day stay in Johannesburg. Close geographically, Johannesburg was a world away from Pretoria in atmosphere. In less than twenty years, the discovery of gold had transformed a stretch of barren veld into a brash, vibrant, cosmopolitan settlement; the Golden City to those who lived there, a sodom and Gomorrah to the Boers who surrounded it. Here, as Princess Christian drove through the lively streets, she was given an uproarious reception. As far as the majority of Johannesburg's citizens were concerned, there was no question that the right side had won the recent war.

Again, although the visit was meant to be a private one, the Princess performed several public duties. She laid the inevitable foundat on stone (this one of a new wing to the Johannesburg Hospital) and presented the King's colours to various regiments.

From the tawny Highveld the royal train went snaking south into the green grasslands of that most royalist of territories, Natal. Here, one of the main attractions for the visitors were the battlefields of the war. Leaving their train both at Dundee and Ladysmith (Princess Christian slipped and fell on the red carpet as she was leaving the Dundee station platform but was quickly on her feet again), they toured the terrain in tented Cape carts. Every now and then they would alight to go striding across the veld, the tubby Princess Christian asking innumerable questions and the skinny Princess Victoria photographing for all she was worth.

In the capital, Pietermaritzburg, things took on a more formal flavour, with Princess Christian presenting more colours and attending a garden party within the red-brick walled garden of Government House. On 6 October, the royal travellers reached Durban. Here there was time for only a triumphant drive through the streets and yet another garden party before they returned to their train for the long haul back to Cape Town. They stopped briefly at

Bloemfontein, which, since the visit of Prince Alfred in 1860, had developed into a city not unlike that other Boer capital, Pretoria: formally set out, graced with handsome public buildings and wearing an air of sleepy respectability.

The princesses reached Cape Town on Sunday 9 October. They had been on the move for exactly a month and had covered some four thousand miles. \ For the first time a member of the British royal family had travelled, albeit privately, through the South African territories now under British sway. It was almost a hundred years since Britain had permanently occupied the Cape in 1806; now the whole of South Africa, from wave-dashed Cape Point to the sultry banks of the Limpopo, was part of the British Empire. As yet, the conquered Boer republics of the Transvaal and the Orange Free State were ruled by Whitehall; the future constitution of the four South African territories had still to be decided. It was generally assumed that South Africa would one day become as unified and self-contained a British colony as Australia or Canada or New Zealand.

And if the journey of King Edward VII's sister through the four as yet un-united states of South Africa had done anything towards emphasising the fact that they would soon all be components of one country, then all to the good. Indeed, a more sympathetic representative of the British monarchy than this sensible, tactful and warm-hearted mother visiting the grave of her son, could hardly have been imagined. Throughout her long journey Princess Christian's behaviour had been conciliatory and circumspect. This was not the time for a triumphal royal tour. Those could, and would, come later.

President Kruger's funeral procession drawn up in Church Square, Pretoria.

5

Less than a month after Princess Christian had sailed home in the *Kildonan Castle*, the body of President Paul Kruger arrived in Cape Town from Europe. From here the coffin was transported to Pretoria. On Friday 16 December (it was one of Afrikanerdom's hallowed dates, for on this day in 1838 the Voortrekkers had gained a great victory over the Zulu nation) the President was buried in the Pretoria cemetery. The air at the graveside was thick with perorations. While General Louis Botha took advantage of the opportunity to urge the unification of all the white people of South Africa, the Rev. H. S. Bosman, the Moderator of the Dutch Reformed Church, urged an even more circumscribed course. He took as his text Psalm 137. Just as the Israelites in captivity had lost their leaders so, he announced, had the Boers. And just as, by putting their faith in the Almighty, the Israelites had been delivered from captivity, so would the Boers be delivered. The body of their great leader might be dead, but his spirit lived on.

Those who imagined that the political aspirations of Afrikanerdom had been buried in Kruger's grave were to be proved very wrong indeed.

The Prince Charming of the 1920s – Edward, Prince of Wales.

THE PRINCE OF WALES

1

NEVER HAD AN HEIR TO THE BRITISH THRONE BEEN MORE popular. If King George V was a somewhat remote figure, his eldest son Edward (or David, as he was known to the family) was anything out remote. In fact, he was only too accessible. For some fifteen years, from the end of the First World War until his accession in 1936, the Prince of Wales was the darling of the British Empire. Slim, slight, good-looking, with an enduring boyishness that belied his years (he turned thirty in 1924), he was a prototype Prince Charming. No international personality was as well known, no country boasted a better roving ambassador, no bachelor in the world was more eligible. Heir to the most firmly established throne in the world, the Prince of Wales nonetheless seemed to epitomise his times: he appeared casual, unconventional, impatient of protocol, and determined to enjoy every minute of the day.

His relatively democratic upbringing, combined with his own independent nature, had ensured this result. Created Prince of Wales in 1911 (it was the year after his father's accession), the young man had led a much less restricted life than any previous heir. At thirteen he had been sent to the Royal Naval College at Osborne. This had been followed by a spell at Dartmouth, where he did not shine, and by a couple of years at Oxford, where he shone even less brightly. At the outbreak of the First World War, the Prince had been attached to the staff of the commander-in-chief of the British Expeditionary Force and had seen service, of a necessarily circumscribed sort, in France. He had returned home, after the Armistice, at the age of twenty-four. Once back, he came face to face with a difficult situation.

If King George V and Queen Mary had made a success of their marriage, as parents they had not been anything like as successful. Both were too undemonstrative, too unbending, too conscious of the prestige of their position, to allow for a warm and uninhibited relationship with their children. With their eldest son, the Prince of Wales, they were on particularly uneasy terms. While he considered their way of life to be too dull and punctilious by half, they considered him to be far too frivolous for his position.

And, in a way, they were right. The Prince of Wales might be the golden boy to those who did not know him well, but he had some serious defects of character. He lacked serious-mindedness. He seldom read, he was not really interested in politics, he avoided anyone who was too scholarly or informed.

He was impulsive, restless, unreliable. Lacking inner resources, he gave himself over to the pursuit of pleasure. He loved parties, practical jokes, fancy dress, in fact, the whole frenetic round of the Jazz Age. Yet, at the same time, he had a strong streak of melancholia; during his ever more frequent black moods he could be petulant and inconsiderate. He was not even as democratic or progressive as he was imagined to be; his apparent enlightenment was merely a reaction to the stuffiness of his father's court. He recoiled, he once claimed, 'from anything that set me up as a person requiring homage'; it was this diffidence in public that led many to believe that he was less concerned with his position than was actually the case.

Having little confidence in his son's abilities, King George V hesitated to involve him in affairs of state. The Prince of Wales, reckoned the King, should confine himself to his traditional duties – laying foundation stones, planting trees and visiting hospitals. But the Prime Minister of the day, David Lloyd George, had other ideas. Fully alive to the Prince's assets (for, whatever his failings, the young man had abundant charm and tireless energy) the Prime Minister decided to make use of them. The Prince of Wales must tour the Empire.

Since the end of the war, the bonds of Empire had shown undeniable signs of slackening; the link between the mother country and the colonies could no longer be taken for granted. These countries were becoming increasingly restive. There was

117

THEO ARONSON

considerable resentment at still being tied, in a fashion, to Britain's apron strings. As yet (and until the signing of the Statute of Westminster in 1931) the various countries making up the Empire were not really autonomous. The idea of a free association of equal partners, united by a common allegiance to the Crown in a British Commonwealth of Nations, had yet to be formulated. But during the 1920s the relationship between Britain and her colonies was changing. What was important was that the one tangible link between these countries – the Crown – be kept intact. Whatever else changed, that must remain.

And what better way of ensuring this than by sending a representative of the monarch to visit these far-flung dominions? A representative, moreover, who was not a staid, old-fashioned and puppet-like princeling, but an informal and engaging young man, very much in tune with a changing world. The monarch himself might be a somewhat unreal figure but his son was exactly the sort of man of whom the honest-to-goodness colonials approved. As Lloyd George once explained to the Prince, 'the appearance of the popular Prince of Wales in far corners of the Empire might do more to calm the discord than half a dozen solemn Imperial Conferences'.

2

And so, for six years, from the age of twenty-five in 1919 until the age of thirty-one in 1925, the Prince of Wales travelled the world. In the course of four mammoth official tours, he visited fifty-five countries and covered 150,000 miles – a distance equal to six circumnavigations of the globe. It was both an exhilarating and an exhausting business. Travel suited his mercurial temperament but the strain on this ever-smiling 'salesman of the Empire' was tremendous. So much of what he had to do was dull routine, yet he was expected to do it with every indication of enjoyment.

'I had come to comprehend as never before', he afterwards wrote, 'the varied burdens of duty that lie upon a Prince of Wales, imposing far greater mental and physical strains than were generally appreciated at the time. Lonely drives through tumultuous crowds, the almost daily inspections of serried ranks of veterans, the inexhaustible supply of cornerstones to be laid, the commemorative trees to be planted, deputations to be met, and everywhere the sad visits to hospital wards, every step bringing me face to face with some inconsolable tragedy calling for a heartening word from me, and always more hands to shake than a dozen Princes could have coped with – such was the substance of my official days.'

No wonder that he could quote the advice of an old courtier as being the soundest he had ever been given: 'Only two rules really count. Never miss an opportunity to relieve yourself; never miss a chance to sit down and rest your feet.'

But it was not all work. The Prince of Wales was never one to pass up a chance of enjoying himself.

Less mature, less disciplined, less conscientious and less dignified than his father had been at his age, and lacking the anchor of a wife, the Prince of Wales was always ready to kick over the traces. And King George V was not the only one to be disturbed by his son's free-and-easy behaviour. The longer the Prince toured, the more frequent were the complaints about his unpunctuality, his rudeness and his lack of consideration. Indeed, there were those who considered the whole of these highly publicised global junketings to be nothing more than a waste of time, effort and money. Or worse still, a valuable opportunity lost.

'Here surely', complained H. G. Wells in the *Review of Reviews,* 'was a chance of saying something that would be heard from end to end of the earth, something kingly and great minded. . . . But from first to last the Prince has said nothing to quicken the imaginations of the multitude of his future subjects to the gigantic possibilities of these times, nothing to reassure the foreign observer that the British Empire embodies anything more than the colossal national egotism of the British people. . . . These smiling tours of the Prince of Wales in these years of shortage, stress, and insecurity, constitute a propaganda of inanity unparalleled in the world's history.'

But on the whole such grumblings were rare. For most of the time, the blond, blue-eyed and wistful-looking Prince moved in an aura of adulation. The world was his oyster and, wherever he went, he was fêted, acclaimed and fawned upon. These years of triumph reached their climax in 1925, when, at the age of thirty, he embarked on his last official tour. It was to be the most significant of his career for it took him to that most politically complicated of all the imperial domains, the Union of South Africa.

3

It was 2 a.m. before the Prince of Wales got to bed on the day that he was due to land in Cape Town – 30 April 1925. There had been a farewell party aboard his ship H.M.S. *Repulse,* at which, runs one report, 'the Prince was the life and soul as well as the principal performer, instrumental and vocal'. Yet at seven-thirty that same morning the Prince was up and dressed, looking as indestructibly boyish as ever and going through the programme of the coming day's events with his comptroller and secretary. From then on, until two-thirty the following morning, when he left the state ball at Government House, he was on the move.

Dressed in the dark-blue uniform of an Admiral of the Fleet and cocked hat, all glittering with gold, the Prince of Wales stepped ashore from the launch that had carried him from the *Repulse* to the city's picturesque pier at the foot of Adderley Street. To meet him were the Governor-General and his wife, both of whom were the Prince's blood relations: the Earl of Athlone was Queen Mary's brother (Prince Alexander of Teck), and the Countess of Athlone was Princess Alice, daughter of Queen Victoria's fourth son, Prince Leopold. Amongst the party of top-hatted, morning-suited and butterfly-collared dignitaries were the South African Prime Minister, General J. B. M. Hertzog, and the leader of the parliamentary opposition, General J. C. Smuts.

The Prince photographed at Government House, Cape Town, with his relations, the Earl and Countess of Athlone.

The handshaking and the small-talk over, there followed a drive through the streets ('I never knew there were so many people in S. Africa as there were filling every street . . .' reported Princess Alice to her sister-in-law Queen Mary); a reception, with speeches, addresses of welcome and more handsnakes, on the Grand Parade; another drive through the acclaiming streets ('Do smile, Sir!' shrieked the girls as they clicked their box-brownies at the gravely saluting Prince); a visit, with a speech to be made, to a gathering of over twenty thousand schoolchildren; a twenty-minute pause at Government House for a change of clothes; a civic luncheon at the City Hall ('another orgy of handshaking – the Prince's arm by this time being nearly nerveless') with more speeches, both to be made and listened to. a further procession ending in a parade of ex-servicemen, scouts and guides, and then an inspect on of a Coloured Church Lads' Brigade.

At five o'clock in the afternoon, with his entourage on a state of near-collapse, the irrepressible Prince suggested a game of golf. The round played, he hurried back to Government House for a further briefing from his secretary, and by eight o'clock, in evening dress, he was presiding over the dinner table at Government House. At the ball which followed he shock hands with every one of the two thousand guests and with as much verve and freshness as if he had never shaken a hand or done a job of work during the whole day', danced almost every dance until he left at two-thirty the following morning.

'David', reported Princess Alice to the Prince's always apprehensive mother, Queen Mary, 'was awfully good, talking to all the right people – indeed there was nothing to criticise. . . .'

It had in fact been a triumphant whirlwind of a day. That the Prince of Wales – so slight, so fresh-faced, so unpretentious and so buoyant – possessed a strong personal magnetism, there was no doubt. 'I had a most uncomfortable sort of lump in the throat, as I watched the Prince and observed his remark-able effect on the whole crowd,' noted one witness of the reception on the Grand Parade. 'Knowing him I knew that it was his own personality that was doing this thing, more than his position as Heir to the British Throne. It is, of course, the combination of his own personality and his position that does the trick, but without that curious personal attraction of his, which is made up of his appearance of youth, his intense humanness, his spontaneity, his absolute lack of all "swank", the mere fact of his being Prince of Wales would not have anything like such a result.'

And the observer was prepared to go further than this. 'To those who are inclined to regard these tours of the Prince of Wales as a formality, or a cer-emonious concession to conventional tradition,' he claimed, 'I would say: Can any elected President do a thing like this, stir to the very heart, individually and collectively, a gathering of people so politically and racially divided as this polyglot concourse on the parade ground at Cape Town? Has the man ever lived who can fuse into one bright flame of imperial fellowship, opposing creeds, different religions, political animosities: melting obstacles, destroying feuds, breaking barriers, uniting enthusiasm, co-ordinating ideals; welding minds and hearts into one great backbone of Empire?'

But it was not, alas, as simple as all that. Not by a long chalk.

4

South Africa, since the visit of Princess Christian two decades before, had undergone considerable constitutional changes. Britain, magnanimous in victory, had lost little time in granting responsible government to the two vanquished Boer republics, and in 1910 the four South African territories – the Cape Colony, Natal, the Transvaal and the Orange Free State – had been welded together to form the Union of South Africa. In November 1910, Queen Victoria's third son, Prince Arthur, Duke of Connaught, had opened the first Union Parliament. The dreams of men like Sir George Grey, Lord Carnarvan and Cecil Rhodes had at last come true.

But this had not, by any means, meant an end of the country's political and racial divisions. In the main, the conflict between the Englishman and the Afrikaner remained unresolved; the emasculated African tribes remained subject peoples; the Coloured people, the Indians and the Malays remained in a sort of racial no-man's-land.

The first prime minister of the new state was that Boer general who had exchanged pleasantries over the luncheon table with Princess Christian – Louis Botha. Assisted by that other one-time Boer general, Jan Smuts, he brought together into one political party – the South African Party – moderate English-speaking and Afrikaans-speaking white South Africans. But the fact that this South African Party professed loyalty to the British Empire proved too much for more nationally minded Afrikaners. Led by yet another general, J. B. M. Hertzog, they formed a party of their own, the National Party. It was not, explained Hertzog, that he was anti-British. He simply saw no reason why the interests of the British Empire should be placed above those of South Africa. What he wanted was a South Africa free from British interference. What the majority of his followers wanted was an independent republic outside the Empire.

On the death of Botha in 1919, Smuts became prime minister. It was he, with his by now firm belief in the value of the imperial connection, who suggested that the Prince of Wales visit South Africa. But in 1924 his South African Party was defeated at the polls by the combined National and Labour parties (strange bedfellows, but in South Africa nothing is ever quite what it seems) and Hertzog became prime minister. For a while it was thought that the royal visit might be cancelled. But it was merely postponed. General Hertzog professed himself quite ready to receive the Prince of Wales.

The Prince, whatever his political limitations, was fully alive to the delicate situation in South Africa. He was in the country as the representative of the British Crown; among his hosts – the government in power – were many who were living for the day when even that purely symbolic link with the Empire could be broken. Thus, at a banquet given in the Houses of Parliament, the Prince delivered an important policy statement on the imperial connection. The speech (which had no doubt been drafted for him in London) has been described as 'the happiest and most valuable' of his tour.

General Hertzog, speaking first, limited himself to assuring the Prince of a warm welcome throughout the country, even in 'the high veld of the Transvaal and the plains of the Free State'. General Smuts, on the other hand, claimed that not only did all sections of the community feel a deep personal affection for the Prince, but they had already shown that they valued the connection with the Crown.

The Prince, who was always nervous before making a speech (he would finger his tie, smooth his fair hair and fiddle with his notes) spoke with great authority that evening. His visits to the other dominions, he said, had opened his eyes to the great development taking place in the constitutional status of the various self-governing parts of the British Commonwealth. This development had been strikingly illustrated by the fact that each dominion had sent its own representative, to sign on its own behalf, to the Peace Conference at Versailles. In addition, each dominion, in its own right, was a member of the League of Nations. And this development towards greater autonomy was going on all the time. The full conception of what was meant by a 'Brotherhood of Free Nations within the Empire' had still to be worked out.

After laying the foundation stone of the new Cape Town University buildings.

'I realise that the welcome which you extend to me is in recognition of the fact that I come to you as the King's eldest son, as Heir to a Throne under which the members of that Commonwealth are free to develop each on its own lines, but all to work together as one. No Government can represent all parties and all nations within the Empire, but my travels have taught me this, that the Throne is regarded as standing for a heritage of common aims and ideals shared equally by all sections, parties, and nations within the Empire.'

If, concluded the Prince, his visit served in any degree to add to a mutual knowledge and co-operation, he would be content. His listeners, bursting into applause, realised that he had not quite finished. Haltingly, and to the delight of the Nationalists, he spoke a sentence in Afrikaans, 'Gentlemen, I am glad to meet you, and I thank you again for your warm welcome.'

The Prince was loudly cheered. If the warmth with which he was greeted by the Nationalists after his speech was any indication, then it had been a triumph indeed. 'Alge' (the Earl of Athlone) 'will have told you what a great impression David made with his speech when he dined with the Senate and members of Parliament,' reported a gratified Princess Alice to Queen Mary, 'and I hear now that this impression is still lasting with the most rabid Nationalists. They were quite delighted with him.'

The *Cape Argus* was no less delighted. 'The speech will be regarded as a landmark in the constitutional history not only of South Africa, but of the Empire, and it may well mark the beginning of a new era in the political history of the Union. It has given members, and especially the Nationalists, a new view towards royalty, which will clear away many doubts and materially contribute towards a better understanding of the great and beneficent part which the Crown plays in promoting the happiness, prosperity and unity of the Empire as a whole.'

Whether the Prince's presence in South Africa would do anything towards reconciling die-hard Nationalist opinion to a continued association with the Crown remained to be seen.

5

The Prince of Wales spent four days in Cape Town. Looking distinctly embarrassed, he was trundled through the streets in an ox wagon as part of the Cape Town University Rag. In a more serious moment, he was installed as Chancellor of the University and then went on to lay the foundation stone of the new University buildings above Groote Schuur. He was driven about the Cape Peninsula (again and again he commented on its beauty) and, one morning before breakfast, climbed Table Mountain. There was lunch under an awning at Groot Constantia and an inspection of the South African training ship, the *General Botha*. He attended a rugby match at Newlands and a race meeting at Kenilworth.

On 4 May he set off from Cape Town on a ten-thousand-mile journey through the country. A special train had been built for the occasion. Painted white, with the South African coat of arms emblazoned on the side of each carriage, it was extremely luxurious. For his own use, the Prince had a drawing-room, a dining-saloon that could seat ten, a study, a sleeping-compartment and a bathroom. With him, in his carriage, travelled his comptroller, his secretary, three equerries and a doctor. In the other carriages

were accommodated six representatives of the South
African government, as well as a small army of detec-
tives, valets, clerks and servants. A second train (a
pilot train which always travelled ahead of the royal
train) carried police, military representatives, journalists, photographers, a post office and the Prince's
six cars with their chauffeurs. Aboard, also, to ensure
a supply of fresh milk, were two cows; the pilot train
was thus always referred to as 'the cow train'.

*The Prince of Wales, on the left, being trundled through the streets of
Cape Town on an ox wagon, as part of the University Rag procession.*

For almost three months, the white train was the
Prince's home. It carried him through the spectacular
mountain scenery of the Western Cape, along part of
the lush Garden Route, across the scrubby Karroo to
Colesberg (where he was the guest of Sir Abe Bailey

on his farm 'Grootfontein'), down, via Cradock, to Port Elizabeth, and through the undulating, mainly English-speaking areas of the Eastern Cape to East London. Turning north again, he crossed the Orange River and travelled through the great plains of the Orange Free State to Bloemfontein; then across into Basutoland and over the precipitous Drakensberg mountains into the green valleys of Natal – to Durban, Zululand and Pietermaritzburg.

From Natal the train steamed north across the Transvaal border, to Swaziland, to the Eastern Transvaal and back to Pretoria, Johannesburg and the burgeoning towns of the Witwatersrand. Then west, through ever more desolate country to Mafeking (from where the Prince travelled by car to Serowe in Bechuanaland) and up into Rhodesia. Here he visited Bulawayo, the mysterious ruins at Zimbabwe, and the awe-inspiring Victoria Falls. The final turning point reached at Broken Hill in Northern Rhodesia, the royal train chugged back southwards across the vast and empty spaces of the veld, through Kimberley and De Aar, and into the enfolding mountains and mid-winter drizzles of the Western Cape.

In the main, this mammoth journey fell into three categories. There were the brief halts at the towns and dorps; there were the three-and four-day-long visits to the cities; and there were the great gatherings of tribal Africans.

At some of the smaller dorps the visit would entail nothing more than a brief halt at some remote siding to allow the small figure in the broad-brimmed hat to greet a handful of people. At the larger towns there would be a drive through the streets (the cars would have been hastily unloaded from the cow train), an address of welcome, a couple of speeches, an inspection of be-medalled ex-servicemen, guides, scouts and schoolchildren, a word with the oldest inhabitant (who invariably remembered the visit of Prince Alfred in 1860) and a visit to a place of special local interest: it could be an ostrich farm, or a sheep farm, or a mine. The Prince would always be the last to board the train and, as it went steaming away across the veld, he would stand on the observation platform, a slight, lonely figure, waving his hand in answer to the wind-wafted cheers. Within a few hours, he would be going through the same performance all over again.

To allow him some exercise, the train would stop in some lonely stretch of veld and, putting on a couple of sweaters and a pair of shorts, the Prince would go jogging for a few miles beside the track. If the train halted for the night near some sizeable settlement, the local inhabitants would organise a dance in the hope that the Prince would attend. He almost always did. The Prince of Wales adored dancing. 'I danced with the man who danced with the girl who danced with the Prince of Wales' was one of the tunes of the period. While the local scout hall reverberated to the sound of a *boereorkes* battling with ragtime, the

Prince would be giving the wives and the daughters of some remote farming community the thrill of their lifetimes. 'The pleasure he gives on these occasions defies description,' wrote one of his aides. 'Half a dozen dances in a district inspire more honest affection for the Prince, and all that he stands for in the common imagination, than do fifty speeches.'

With this estimate of things, the Prince's father, King George V, could not agree. 'I see David continues to dance every night and most of the night too,' he grumbled to Queen Mary. 'What a pity they should telegraph it every day, people who don't know, will begin to think that he is either mad or the biggest rake in Europe, such a pity!'

If the halting-place were too remote for even an informal dance, the irrepressible Prince would suggest a 'sing-song in the cow train.' While one of the photographers played the piano, the Prince would strum his beloved ukulele. If this sounded too thin, he would start banging a couple of brass trays with his feet. Once, on a type of mouth-organ called a 'gassoon', he gave a dead-pan rendering of the most frequently heard tune of the tour – 'God Bless the Prince of Wales'.

In the cities, things took on a more formal but no less predictable pattern than in the towns. On the beflagged platform the Prince would be met by the berobed mayor and his councillors. There would be a procession through the clamorous streets, a reception under the portico of the city hall, the wreath laid on the war memorial, the inevitable inspection of ex-servicemen, guides, and scouts, a garden party or a race meeting or a schoolchildren's rally, a banquet, a ball and, at well after midnight, a strange bed in a strange government house.

'The programme', wrote the Prince of Wales of one of these tours, 'was my master; I did my best to obey. Two days here, three days there, any number of one-night stands – much of the time I was like a man caught in a revolving door.'

Each city, none the less, had its own atmosphere and its own particular point of interest. Port Elizabeth, at that time regarded as the 'Liverpool of South Africa', was memorable, among other reasons, for the fact that the Prince was obliged to shake hands with over four thousand people before the opening of the ball in the Feather Market Hall. In Bloemfontein, that four-square capital of the Orange Free State, he was escorted by a Boer Commando under the leadership of one of the Boer War generals. In Durban, looking its exotic, mid-winter best ('Durban', wrote one of his entourage, 'is English, with a Scotch accent and an Eastern breath. . . . It was different from any place the Prince had seen before, yet it reminded him of a dozen places he had seen on previous tours'), the Prince opened a new graving-dock. On addressing a gathering of the Indian community in Hindustani, he was told, firmly, that their language was English. In Pietermaritzburg, the red-brick capital of Natal, he opened the Royal Agricultural Show.

Beneath the elegant colonnades of the Union Buildings in Pretoria, he listened to the Pretoria Choral Society singing 'Land of Hope and Glory'. 'There could have been no more wonderful demonstration', wrote one over-optimistic witness, 'of how the differences of over a quarter of a century ago have healed.' In Johannesburg, which the Prince described as 'the great, boisterous, gold-mining city', he toured the Reef and went down a mine. On the following day – 23 June 1925 – he was to turn thirty-one, and the Johannesburg crowds shouted 'Many Happy Returns' as he drove through the streets. From Bulawayo he visited the grave of Cecil John Rhodes, and in Salisbury, that spacious capital of Southern Rhodesia, he was given one of the most tumultuous welcomes of his tour. In Kimberley he was shown over a diamond mine and was driven out to see the Anglo-Boer War battlefield at Magersfontein.

And for most of the time the Prince of Wales remained charming, unflurried, inexhaustible and apparently interested in whatever was being shown to him. 'My God! He's marvellous,' exclaimed one harassed pressman. Only rarely was he seen to lose his composure in public. One such occasion was at a gathering of schoolchildren. They were singing a hymn and, for some reason, the Prince that day found the sound of their shrill and earnest voices particularly stirring. His entourage could sense that the Prince was deeply moved. As the last notes of the hymn died away on the sunlit air, there came

136

a moment of complete and dramatic silence. It was broken by a woman who dashed up to the Prince. 'Won't you please sign your name in this for me, Sir?' she gushed, thrusting an autograph book at him.

For a few seconds the Prince stared at her. 'No,' he said suddenly, 'I will NOT sign your book.'

6

The Prince of Wales's tour saw something like a dozen great African tribal gatherings. These ceremonies were probably the most spectacular, as well as the most delusive, of the royal visit.

By the 1920s, the position of the indigenous peoples of South Africa was a curious one. With all attempts to maintain peaceful frontiers between black and white having come to nothing, successive governments had simply broken the power of the various tribes and annexed their territories. Here, under fairly benevolent European control, the tribesmen lived the life of subject races. In a way, they were colonists of colonists.

Increased economic expansion, however, had led to a drift of the Africans to the towns and cities. Here, despite their absorption into the industrial life of the country, they were still subject peoples. To ensure that they remained so – and that they should constitute no threat to the white workers – legislation was passed to prevent the Africans from competing with the whites on equal terms. At the time of the Prince of Wales's

visit, the National-Labour government, amidst much
political agitation ('Workers of the world, fight and
unite for a White South Africa!' ran what must have
been one of the most extraordinary slogans in the
history of a political movement), was preparing to
strengthen this discriminatory legislation. In 1926,
the controversial Colour Bar Act would be passed.

Denied full economic rights, the Africans were
being denied full political rights as well. Only in the
Cape Colony were certain Africans on the common
electoral roll. This Hertzog and his National Party
were doing their utmost to abolish: Africans must
be removed from the roll and be given separate
representation. During the 1920s his attempts to
achieve this were defeated by a lack of the necessary two-thirds majority in parliament; only in 1936,
with the somewhat hesitant acquiescence of Smuts,
was Hertzog able to remove the Africans from the
common roll.

Thus, at the time of the Prince of Wales's visit in
1925, the question of black-white relations was unresolved. All the brave talk – of democracy and equal-
ity and independence – which so filled the air that
autumn, was meant to apply to the white community
only. With the Africans in the cities – the semi-edu-
cated, industrialised proletariat living in slum condi-
tions on the fringes of the white communities – the
Prince had very little contact. He saw the Africans as
most Europeans preferred to see them, as a simple,
unspoilt, staunchly cribal people content to brew

their beer, herd their cattle, hoe their fields and shake their heads in wonder at the superiority of the white man's ways.

The Prince walks beside a row of chanting Swazi warriors in Mbabane, Swazilana.

And the great *indabas* of the Prince's tour confirmed this view. Whether at Umtata in the Transkei, Eshowe in Zululand, Maseru in Basutoland, Mbabane in Swazi and, Pietersourg in the Transvaal, Serowe in Bechuanaland, Salisbury in Rnodesia; whether they were Xhosa or Zulu or Basuto or Swazi or Shangaan or Bechuana or Matabele, the pattern was largely the same. Under an awring the Prince of Wales would stand, resplendent in spiked white helmet, scarlet tunic, broad blue Garter ribbon, 'absolutely laden with gold lace and jeweled decorations', his hand resting on the hilt of his sword. Stretching before him, as far as he could see, would be thousands upon thousands of tribesmen, hardly less resplendent in ostrich plumes, beads, animal skins, assegais, knobkerries and hide shields. For days and weeks they would have tramped the surrounding hills and valleys in order to render homage to 'The Son of the Great White Chief from over the Water'. The entire scene would represent, as one sycophantic witness put it, 'An Emperor with a back nation at his feet. H.R.H. doing the job of Empire.'

There would be a thunderous greeting, a seemingly interminable intoning of praises, the Prince's speech in which he would remind his listeners of the virtues of 'discipline, of loyalty to those in authority over them', the exchange of gifts (skins and shields for the Prince, silver-headed walking-sticks for the chiefs) and a stamping, chanting, incredibly energetic dance by the assembled warriors. Indeed, so frenziedly aid the Zulu warriors perform their dance that it seemed as though they were about to plunge their assegais into the brightly uniformed little Prince. 'A rotten kind of finish for H.R.H.,' mused one of his aides.

A thrust of another sort, however, was made by Solomon ka Dinizulu, the senior Zulu chief. For once, a speech was not all platitudinous praise. 'But we are Zulu,' he proclaimed. 'A nation of men. Every free nation has the right to make its own laws. O Prince, we claim that right. It is our hope that we may be allowed to exercise that right in the future.'

The plea was significant. An African chief was addressing himself directly to the representative of the British monarch above the heads of the South

African administration. Denied what he considered to be his true rights, Solomon was appealing to one who, in theory, was set in authority over the South African government.

His Royal Highness, totally unprepared for this plunge into constitutional niceties, stuck doggedly to his prepared text in his speech.

Nor did the day's embarrassments end there. To many of the Europeans attending the ceremony it seemed as though the traditional greeting cries of *Bayete!* were being given to Chief Solomon and not to the Prince of Wales. That this was a case of 'studied rudeness' to the Prince on the part of the Zulu chief, the *Natal Mercury,* for one, had no doubt. Bristling with monarchist indignation, the newspaper endorsed a demand that 'some steps should be taken to administer a reproof to Solomon which will be understood not only by the Chief himself but also by the whole Zulu nation'. With Solomon denying that any dishonour had been intended, the argument became increasingly heated. It ended only after the Chief had sued the *Natal Mercury* for libel and was granted damages. Denied economic and political rights, the Africans were at least able to enjoy full legal rights.

7

How much truth there is in the often-repeated stories of the Prince's sexual escapades while in South Africa, one does not know. It is difficult to see how he could

have found the time, or the opportunity, for anything but the briefest flirtation. He hardly ever had
a moment to himself; he was constantly surrounded,
not only by equerries and police, but by hordes of
people; he never stayed in any one place for more
than three or four days. Even his spare time seems
to have been devoted to rounds of golf or chukkas
of polo.

He was, of course, extremely attractive to women;
and would have been so without his winsome looks.
The Prince, in turn, was attracted to them. Often, at
the cost of offending some dignitary's overdressed and
rigidly corseted wife, he would lead someone younger
and prettier onto the dance floor. He was known to
dance half-a-dozen dances in succession with the same
girl or even to arrange for her to come on to a dance
to which she had not been invited. 'But, on the other
hand,' says a member of his entourage, 'I have never
seen him disappear with her out of sight and range of
everybody . . and I have never heard of his doing so –
from anyone who has any first-hand knowledge.'

This may well have been true; in South Africa, at
least. In England it would have been another matter.
On tour, with the public spotlight always upon him, it
would have been all but impossible for the Prince to
enjoy even the most hurried liaison. He would never,
one knows, have lacked willing partners. Girls flung
themselves at him (two of them, having danced with
him in Canada and the United States respectively, followed him to South Africa in the hopes of yet another

foxtrot) and, given the opportunity, the Prince might have availed himself of it.

On the other hand, the Prince of Wales was never as great a lover as was generally supposed. His taste was for married women, more particularly if they were of a motherly, somewhat domineering type; throughout this period he was known to be deeply in love with Mrs Freda Dudley Ward. The truth was that few could believe that so romantic and sought-after a figure should not avail himself of every opportunity to satisfy his desires. The wish was indeed father to the thought in this case. Certainly the legend of his sexual promiscuity lived on in South Africa and, for years after the visit, proud husbands would claim that their sons, or daughters, had been fathered by the Prince of Wales.

When, on one occasion, opportunity of a sort did present itself, the Prince was thrown into a quandary. His train had been drawn up for the night beside some lonely siding in the veld when an African approached and asked to see the Prince. He wished, he explained politely, to make a gift of his seventeen-year-old daughter to the Prince. 'Now what on earth am I going to do about this?' asked the Prince of his companions. It was decided that he would grant the African an audience, accept his gift by placing his hands on the girl's head, and repay the gift by presenting the girl, plus six fat oxen, back to the father.

The arrangement delighted everyone. Everyone, that is, except the girl, who burst into tears at her rejection. Sobbing bitterly, she followed her gratified father back home through the darkening veld.

But it was rarely that any encounter with the Prince of Wales ended in tears. On some his presence could have an uplifting, almost mystical effect. He was reputed, rightly or wrongly, to have boundless sympathy with those in suffering. The story used to be told of how, when faced with a man who had been blinded, deafened and struck dumb during the war, the Prince bent and kissed his mutilated cheek. And on another occasion, he is said to have entered a miner's cottage in order to hold the hand of his wife in the agony of childbirth.

Young Cecile Smith of Port Alfred, forced to break off her studies at the Teachers' Training College in Grahamstown because of a severe illness, had a similar story to tell. Her bed had been carried out onto the verandah of her father's home in Port Alfred so that she might see the Prince drive by. As he passed, he raised his broad-brimmed hat and smiled. The following evening, she was astonished to hear that the Prince, having noticed that she was in bed, had called to see her. Her father led him into the room, and there, for fifteen minutes, the Prince brought the sick girl untold joy by chatting quietly to her of his visit to the Training College the day before and of his games of golf on the local course.

For her it was unforgettable. 'In fact,' she says, 'that time seemed to be the turning-point of my illness, for since then I have made rapid strides towards recovery. Now I am able to take a few steps and am feeling just ever so much better.'

8

That was one side of the coin. There was another, hardly less typical, side. For this Prince, who could be so gracious and considerate, could also be brusque and arrogant.

While in the Orange Free State, the Prince spent a few days on the South African estate of the Duke of Westminster, not far from the Basutoland border. He was hoping to play some polo, for which, says one of his party, he was 'absolutely gasping'. But the rain pelted down throughout his stay. Almost entirely lacking in mental resources, the Prince became increasingly bored and fretful. However, a dance had been arranged for one evening and a few people had been invited to dine at the house beforehand.

Among them was a spirited young woman by the name of Marjorie Juta. Despite the relentlessly pouring rain, she and a friend set out from a nearby farm. With the dirt roads awash, it would have been impossible to go by car; the two young women therefore decided to take a dog cart. Dressed in jodhpurs and greatcoats and with their evening dresses in a tarpaulin-covered suitcase under the seat, they jolted and slithered their way along the rain-dark road. By the time they reached the Duke of Westminster's house, they were wet through. Only the thought of meeting the most romantic figure in the world had kept up their spirits.

They were greeted at the door by the Duke's agent. The sight of these two bedraggled creatures in outsize army greatcoats vastly amused him. 'By Jove, this is sporting of you!' he exclaimed. 'H.R.H. will be delighted. Do come and meet him. It'll amuse him no end.'

It amused him not at all. Nor did he show the slightest interest in the predicament of these two rain-drenched women. He simply muttered, 'How-do-you-do,' and went on with his cocktail. The crestfallen arrivals were led away to bath and change.

At dinner the Prince, as Marjorie Juta puts it, 'drank a great deal more than he ate'. By the end of the meal he appeared to be drunk. In the Daimler, on the way to the dance in the local school hall, he confined himself to playing his ukulele. Arrived at the dance, he converted, as one of his fawning aides puts it, 'a damp and doleful evening into a particularly bright and successful one', by twirling a coloured umbrella and singing 'It ain't gonna rain no mo'.

In fact, he converted that damp and doleful evening into a particularly stormy one by becoming more petulant still and by insisting on dancing with his chauffeur's girl friend. The chauffeur became increasingly angry, the Prince became increasingly possessive, and only by holding the irate chauffeur back could the Prince's companions prevent H.R.H. from being beaten up.

'We returned', says Marjorie Juta tactfully, 'a little chastened to our home.'

9

Two men particularly impressed the Prince of Wales during his South African tour. The one, of course, was General Smuts. The tour, the Prince afterwards wrote, had 'given me a measure of the greatness of Smuts himself, who almost alone of the old Boer leaders worked ceaselessly and hopefully to hold South Africa within the Empire'. The other was the Minister of Posts, the Labour member, Thomas Boydell.

High-spirited, English-born and relatively young, Tommy Boydell stood out in sharp contrast to the older and possibly more dour Nationalist cabinet ministers. He was in attendance on the Prince for much of the tour and made a great appeal, both as a raconteur and a practical joker. Once the Prince bet him that he would never dare to be photographed alone with a lion. That very evening Boydell presented the Prince with a photograph of himself stroking a large lion. He had borrowed the docile beast from a travelling circus.

On another occasion, when the Prince told Boydell that he would very much like to return to

South Africa on an unofficial visit, the Minister suggested that the Prince come out under another name.

'What name do you suggest?' asked the Prince.

'Fourie, Sir,' answered Tommy Boydell unhesitatingly.

'But why, of all your names, Fourie?' asked the Prince.

'Because,' explained Boydell unblinkingly, 'wherever you go you hear the people singing, "Fourie's a jolly good fellow".'

10

Throughout his three months in South Africa, the Prince of Wales paid particular attention to one of his main tasks: he did his utmost to please the Afrikaners. His personality – his approachability and informality – ensured that he would win one half of the battle; by a conciliatory attitude he hoped to win the other.

His speech at the parliamentary banquet in Cape Town had already done a great deal of good, and from then on, in all his speeches, he referred to the necessity of a more harmonious relationship between the two white races. He visited that seedbed of Afrikaner nationalism, the University of Stellenbosch, and delighted the students. He attempted, with unspectacular results, to learn Afrikaans by taking instruction from a specially appointed Afrikaans-speaking A.D.C., Leonard Beyers. Gamely, he would ask for a horse and go cantering into some country town in the middle of a ragged, slouch-hatted commando. He dutifully laid wreaths on the graves of Britain's old enemies – President Kruger, President Steyn and President Pretorius.

How effective any of this was is difficult to judge. The leader-writers in English language newspapers were certainly full of the benefits to be reaped from the Prince's visit. 'South Africa has seen and learned', enthused one of them, 'that our Monarchical system is no affair of rattling sabres and shining armour. . . . May we not now say, with confidence, that the old meaning of Empire, wherein seemed to lurk a menace to freedom-loving people, has finally vanished from the veld in the presence of the Prince and with his coming?'

The Prince of Wales, heir to the British throne, pays tribute to the memory of President Paul Kruger, in the Pretoria cemetery.

Surely, argued another, those who still dreamed of a republic could now see how democratic, how unpompous and how pliable was the British monarchical system. Surely, by the presence of this easygoing and forward-looking Prince, something definite had been done to keep South Africa in the Empire. 'If, under the Empire, is a scheme of things which guarantees freedom and makes for the full realisation of national life, is a Republic really called for?'

But the writers were allowing themselves to be carried away. The Prince may have won some esteem but it is doubtful whether he changed any opinions. 'Prince,' exclaimed one Nationalist member teasingly after the Prince had made his speech to the parliamentarians, 'we want you to stay here with us and be our first President.' In other words, they liked him for himself and not as the representative of the British Crown. In fact, it did not take the Prince long to realise that the gap between the two white factions was almost unbridgeable. In Johannesburg, a Nationalist cabinet minister refused to be seen driving beside him through the streets and, on another occasion, yet another cabinet minister (Oxford educated) declared that the Afrikaner would never forgive the British for their unwarranted attack on the two Boer republics.

'But surely,' asked the Prince, 'this bitterness will eradicate itself as the generations move further away from that war?'

'No, Sir,' answered the minister emphatically, 'never.'

And, as far as some Afrikaners were concerned, he was right. For them, there would be no rest until the link with Britain was completely broken. In 1931, when, largely at the instigation of General Hertzog, Britain by the Statute of Westminster granted her ex-colonies Dominion Status (thus ensuring virtual independence for South Africa), Hertzog felt that the battle had been won. Republicanism, he declared, was no longer an important issue; only by the Crown was South Africa now linked to the British Commonwealth.

But a great number of his fellow Nationalists could not agree. Even that symbolic link, they claimed, must go. Again the Afrikaners split and in 1934 Dr D. F. Malan formed the Purified National Party. It was a party dedicated to the establishment of a republic, quite independent of the British Crown.

11

On 29 July 1925, H.M.S. *Repulse* sailed away from Cape Town. Some ten weeks later, after a visit to South America, the Prince of Wales arrived home. The last of his great Empire tours was over. His education, as someone put it, had been completed 'on the trade routes of the world'.

Whatever the value of this education, it was not put to any use once the Prince reached home. For the following decade the Prince of Wales was obliged to play the thankless role of a King-in-Waiting, a position 'which at times seemed to leave me dangling futilely in space between the ceremonial make-believe symbolising the power of high and mighty princes and the discouraging realities of a world that insisted upon relegating even a conscientious Prince to a figure-head role'.

Gradually, the golden prince of the 1920s developed into the somewhat tarnished figure of the 1930s. Ageing, unmarried, unemployed, immature, the Prince of Wales seemed to be leading a worthless existence. There were grumblings about his not settling down, about his not taking life seriously enough. 'What is excusable and of course natural in a youth', wrote one disapproving journalist, 'can be disquieting in a man.' Disquieting it certainly was, and more disquieting still it became, until, in 1936, after his accession to the throne as King Edward VIII, the news of his determination to marry the twice-divorced Wallis Simpson burst upon the Empire.

Among the Dominion prime ministers consulted on the question of the King's – possibly morganatic – marriage was the South African prime minister, General Hertzog. In common with all the others, Hertzog could not agree to the King's both marrying and retaining his throne. While abdication, replied Hertzog, would be a 'great shock', a morganatic marriage would be 'a permanent wound'. To answers such as this, King Edward VIII complained that no attempt had been made to assess public opinion in the dominions; surely those years of touring had left behind a fund of goodwill towards him? Surely somewhere in the prairie or bush or veld he had defenders?

But whether he had or not was by now immaterial. On 11 December 1936, King Edward VIII abdicated his throne to marry Mrs Simpson. His brother, Prince Albert, Duke of York, ascended the throne as King George VI.

THE ROYAL FAMILY

1

IT WAS A PERFECT SUMMER DAY. THE SUN WAS HOT, THE AIR was still, the sky was cloudless. Table Mountain looked, according to one lyrical observer, as 'clean-cut as a painting by Canaletto'. Since dawn on that 17 February 1947, the Cape Town crowds had been lining the streets of the city and filling the stands that had been especially erected on the foreshore – that recently reclaimed stretch of land between the sea and the city. On the glittering waters of Table Bay lay the vast grey battleship, H.M.S. *Vanguard*. The gold and red and blue of the royal standard, rippling in the slight breeze, indicated that the Sovereign was aboard. King George VI, accompanied by Queen Elizabeth and their two daughters, Princess Elizabeth and Princess Margaret, was about to embark on the first state visit of a British sovereign to South Africa.

On a circular, canopied, red-carpeted dais on the quayside were collected a huddle of dignitaries, headed by the Governor-General, Gideon Brand van Zyl, and the Prime Minister, Field-Marshal Smuts. At half past eight, as the *Vanguard* started to move slowly towards the dock, four small figures emerged to take their places on a platform high above the huge guns of the forward turret. As the Queen raised her hand in characteristic greeting, a great roar went up from the crowd on the quay.

With the ship berthed, the Governor-General, followed by Smuts and various military personel, went on board to greet the visitors and to submit, in symbolic fashion, their delegated authority to their Sovereign. After a brief exchange they returned ashore to take up their places at the foot of the red-carpeted gangplank. To the clashing of anthems (both 'God Save the King' and 'Die Stem van Suid Afrika'), the thunder of guns and the cheering of the crowd, the royal family stepped ashore.

To many of the thousands upon thousands of people collected in Cape Town that sweltering day, the appearance of the royalties, in person, came as something of a surprise. One woman radio commentator, astonished at the sight of them, went so far as to exclaim that they were beautiful, beautiful people. And so, in a way, they were. Most South Africans had been quite unprepared for the glamour of the royal family. At the time when the reproduction of colour photography was still comparatively rare, the public were accustomed to seeing the family pictured in black and white. They had usually been shown in some wartime setting (for the Second World War had been over for only eighteen months) with the King in a dark uniform and the Queen in a simple off-the-face hat, inspecting bomb sites or troops or rows of nurses. In addition, none of the members of the family were particularly photogenic.

Now, seen in the flesh, in so sunny and exhilarating a setting, they had an almost technicolour quality about them. The fifty-one-year-old King George VI, in his white uniform of an Admiral of the Fleet, with its sparkling gold braid, badges and buttons, looked surprisingly handsome: bronzed, blue-eyed, boyishly slender. The forty-six-year-old Queen Elizabeth looked superb. Her particularly Celtic looks – her marshmallow complexion, her bright-blue eyes, her jet-black hair – were enlivened by the most radiant of smiles. She was dressed with great panache. Her hat was a tilted, towering concoction of mist-blue ostrich feathers; more feathers fringed the panels that floated from the shoulders to the hem of her matching mist-blue dress. About her throat gleamed three ropes of pearls.

If the two princesses did not wear clothes with their mother's assurance – they were in simple, girlish dresses – they too, were more attractive than had been supposed. Both had clear, peaches-and-cream complexions and dazzling smiles. Of the two, the sixteen-year-old Princess Margaret had the livelier, more piquant face; Princess Elizabeth, at twenty, could look grave. But all in all, they made an engaging family group, fresh, well groomed and with a lustre that was not entirely due to their rank.

The formal greetings at the quayside over, the family drove in open cars through the streets of the city. Cape Town, by now, was a city of some half-a-million people; it seemed, on that sunlit morning, as though they must all be out in the streets. Their cheering was thunderous. The royal family, who had been warned that the South Africans were not a demonstrative people, were delighted with their reception. From the glaring sunshine of the streets, the procession moved into the shade of Government Avenue, and the royal party alighted at the white gates of Government House. The specially renovated building was to be their home during their stay in Cape Town.

*Beneath the guns of H.M.S. Vanguard, the royal family pose
in a domestic group, on the voyage out to South Africa.*

The four and a half days spent in the city were crowded with engagements. In the white and gold ballroom of Government House the King accepted a loyal address from the members of the two Houses of Parliament and presented a delighted Field-Marshal Smuts with the Order of Merit. They attended a state banquet in the City Hall ('As the Queen walked in, a murmur could be heard, because she really looked magnificent,' wrote one of the guests) and at this banquet the King, who was known to have once suffered from a speech impediment, surprised his apprehensive audience by the strength and clarity of his voice. On the Grand Parade they were officially welcomed to the Cape Province, in halting English, by the Administrator, the Hon. J.G.Carinus, and to the city of Cape Town by the Mayor, Abe Bloomberg. (The Mayor's address of welcome was considered highly effective; indeed, in Abe and Miriam Bloomberg, the city had a particularly stylish and accomplished mayoral couple.) It was at this reception on the Parade that the Queen first broke the set procedure in order to go and speak to a group of wounded ex-servicemen. Such spontaneous gestures were to be repeated again and again during the tour.

There was a garden party on the lawns of Westbrook, the Governor-General's official country house; there was a civic ball in the City Hall, at which the guests, in an enraptured, apparently immovable mass, stood gazing up at the royal box; there was a drive through rows of cheering schoolchildren (neatly and firmly segregated into races, noted the visiting journalists) to Simonstown. When the Mayor of Simonstown presented the customary golden book for the royal signatures, Smuts, that one-time Boer general, greatly amused the King by leaning forward to say, 'You must do this, you know, as this is the spot where you first attacked us, so at least you must do something to restore the damage.'

At Kenilworth race course, the Queen and her daughters bet successfully on the favourite; at the Joint Parliamentary Sports Meeting at Fernwood, the Queen, with that blend of charm and astuteness, tried her hand at the exclusively Afrikaner game of *jukskei*; at a ball given for the Coloured community in the City Hall, the fascinated family stayed much longer than had been intended. 'These coloured folk', decided one British journalist, 'were an ebulliently cheerful people, who managed their entertainment with better organisation and took their pleasures far more gaily than their European counterparts the night before.'

The fourth day – Thursday 20 February – took the family, for the first time, into an atmosphere that was rather less ebullient. They drove that day, through magnificent mountain scenery, into the vineyards of Paarl and Stellenbosch. At Paarl they sampled that characteristically South African institution of the morning tea party and had lunch, *al fresco,* at the beautiful farm 'Bien Donné'. In the afternoon they visited Stellenbosch for yet another tea party. And it was here, contrary to the optimistic claims of the English-language press, that the family experienced a somewhat restrained reception. British journalists with the party noticed that, although the welcome was respectful, it was in no way ecstatic.

The afternoon came as a reminder that it was not to be roses quite all the way and that there was an underlying reason for this royal visit.

2

Field-Marshal Smuts had high hopes of the royal tour. South Africa by 1947 was emerging from one of its most difficult political periods. The outbreak of the Second World War had finally put an end to the always uneasy alliance between Smuts and Hertzog. Smuts, on a slender parliamentary majority, had taken South Africa into the war as an ally of Great Britain, leaving the disapproving Hertzog to form the small Afrikaner Party. Throughout the war, the main opposition party – the National Party headed by Malan – maintained a sympathetic attitude towards Germany. This surely was their chance: a German victory over the British would mean that South Africa could become a republic. There was no open rebellion, but Smuts was obliged to fight the war with one eye over his shoulder.

THEO ARONSON

Smuts and the King

But if, by the end of the war, South Africa had emerged from one difficult period, she was entering another infinitely more difficult one. Smuts might be a figure of great international stature but he was not anything like as highly regarded at home. To some, he seemed incapable of applying himself to the problems of his own country. On the most pressing problem, that of relations between black and white, he seemed to have no clear-cut policy. A war just having been fought in defence of democracy, the Africans and Asians saw no reason why this democracy should not now be extended to them. Smuts, heading the United Party, whose members ranged from liberals to arch-reactionaries, was in a difficult position. Perhaps he hoped that, with enough goodwill, things would somehow work themselves out.

162

The National Party, on the other hand, knew its own mind perfectly. It wanted a complete separation of the black and white races and it wanted a republic. And by playing on the racial fears of the white population, as well as their post-war discontents, the Nationalists were gaining ground. A general election was due in 1948; perhaps the Nationalists could tip the scales their way.

To help keep them tipped his way was one of the reasons why Smuts invited the royal family to South Africa. By now this one-time republican was an ardent – some of his enemies said a sycophantic – monarchist. He had considerable faith in the power of royalty to influence public opinion. 'This is just the sort of thing which Kings and Queens can do and which give them a blessed and fruitful function in our human society. . . .' he claimed. 'Nowhere is it more wanted than in this land of races and colours, and nowhere can it render a greater service. Politics runs too high with us, and as the King is above all politics he becomes the reconciler and the peacemaker.'

It was certainly an idealistic and, in the event, an optimistic conception of the role of the monarchy. And what gave Smuts greater faith still in the potency of the Crown was the personalities of the visiting royalties. Surely in the face of this charming family – the unassuming King, the friendly Queen, the unspoilt princesses – some of the opposition to the concept of monarchy would melt. Who could possibly resent such kindly, well-meaning people? What republican could withstand the Queen's smile? The news of the tour, he maintained, was received by 'our South African people with an enthusiasm that exceeded even my most optimistic expectations. . . . The clamour to see the Royal Family was loud and insistent – and it came from every part of the population.'

What had originally been intended as a much-needed post-war holiday for King George VI was expanded into a full-scale tour of the country. This first visit of a reigning sovereign, this climax to all the previous royal tours, was to be put to its most effective use. At times, the pace would be little short of gruelling. February can be the hottest month in South Africa, and for day after day, for weeks on end, the royal family would be obliged to fulfil an exhausting round of public engagements. The Queen was to admit to her mother-in-law, Queen Mary, that the tour was 'very strenuous'; the King was to lose a stone in weight. It was a wonder that they could do it all so gracefully and so uncomplainingly.

King George VI's most important single task was to open the new session of the Union Parliament. Hitherto, the South African Parliament had always been opened in his name by the Governor-General; on this occasion, the presence of the Sovereign would both highlight and personalise the link between South Africa and the Crown. King George VI would be opening Parliament, not as the visiting King of England, but as the King of South Africa. It was a significant occasion, not only for South Africa, but for the rest of the Commonwealth, for this would be the

first time that the Sovereign would be opening a parliament outside Great Britain. h ceremony would
dramatise the relationship between the monarchy
and the dominions.

*Preceded by Group-Captain Peter Townsend, the
King and Queen leave the Houses of Parliament,
Cape Town, after the official opening.*

The ceremony, performed on Friday 21 February 1947 in the Senate Chamber of the Houses of Parliament in Cape Town, was brilliantly successful. Both the King and the Queen wore white, dramatically slashed, in each case, by the broad blue Garter ribbon. The King's naval uniform glittered with braid and decorations; the Queen's dress was sewn with blue and silver and aquamarine brilliants, and on her dark hair flashed a magnificent tiara. The King read his speech from the Throne and, having declared Parliament open in English, did the same in halting Afrikaans. 'Most people would have been tempted to garble the Afrikaans wording, noted one of the cabinet ministers, 'but he struggled through, pronouncing each word as well as he could, while all precedent was . . . broken by the low murmur of approval, which ran like a whisper through the crowd.'

Few would forget the sight of the royal couple descending the steps of the Houses of Parliament at the close of the ceremony. Slowly, between rows of motionless troops presenting arms, they came: the King erect and grave, the Queen dignified but smiling, with the embroidered panels that fell from her shoulders forming a long train behind her.

3

Within the first few days of the royal visit, it had become apparent that the Queen was emerging as the most remarkable member of the family.

King George VI, although in many ways an admirable man, lacked public presence. By the time he visited South Africa in 1947, he had been on the throne for over a decade, yet he remained a somewhat unimpressive figure. The abdication of his brother, King Edward VIII, had suddenly thrust him into a position for which he had not been adequately trained; nor did he have the necessary personal qualifications for the showier aspects of his task. He was shy, insecure, diffident; he had never quite conquered his youthful stammer. Genial and relaxed in private company, he appeared ill at ease in public. He often looked preoccupied; he seemed incapable of making a spontaneous gesture. Nor was his health particularly good. He had never been strong and the strain of his position was taking its toll. During this South African tour he often suffered severe pain from a duodenal ulcer.

Causing the King additional concern on this tour were the sufferings of the British population during a particularly cruel winter. There was even some criticism of the fact that, while his people shivered, the King was holidaying in the sun. So strongly did he feel this unjust criticism that he at one stage contemplated cutting short his tour and returning home. The British Prime Minister, Clement Attlee, advised against this.

Yet, however hesitant or worried King George might sometimes look in public, he was both a conscientious and a courageous man. Temperamentally unsuited for his task, he none the less forced himself to do it as well as he possibly could. He never shirked a duty. Few men could have worked harder to make a success of a job which they did not really enjoy.

The princesses, too, at this stage of their lives, lacked strong public images. Having led somewhat secluded lives during the war, this was their first exposure to the sustained public gaze; never before had they been so continuously and so mercilessly on show. Princess Elizabeth, who had inherited her father's shyness, sometimes appeared rather stolid. Princess Margaret, although more vivacious and already showing signs of what would one day be considerable beauty, still suffered from some of the gaucherie – and impishness – of youth.

But the Queen was different. The days when she had been known as 'the little Duchess' – a small, somewhat insignificant-looking member of the British royal family – had long since passed. By now, Queen Elizabeth had come well and truly into her own. These years, from the end of the Second World War until the death of the King in 1952, were to be her most spectacular. The South African tour was to see the Queen in full flower.

Short, plump and pretty, Queen Elizabeth could none the less give off an indefinable aura of majesty. Some, at least, of this aura was due to the way she dressed. On her state visit to Paris before the war, the French had said that, although she was not chic, she dressed like a queen. And this was true. Like Queen Alexandra and Queen Mary before her, Queen

Elizabeth had developed, and remained faithful to, her own particular style. It had little to do with fashion, but everything with effect. This gave it the advantage of never looking dated.

By day she wore hydrangea shades – pale pinks, blues and mauves – with her hats matching her dresses so that, by wearing a single pastel shade, she always stood out in a crowd. Her hats were elaborate, height-giving confections of feathers or flowers or veiling; her dresses, with their floating panels or their straight-cut, matching coats were designed to give an illusion of slimness and an added dignity. At a time of knee-length skirts, she wore hers to the calf; her heels were always high. The result was that, in the flesh, she always appeared taller and slimmer than she actually was. At night, in crinolines of satin and tulle, lavishly embroidered, and with diamonds sparkling about her neck and on her black hair, she looked breathtaking. She could never be mistaken for anything other than a queen.

To this striking appearance the Queen brought a complete ease of manner. She was dignified but, more important, she was assured, never at a loss for the right word, the appropriate gesture or the correct procedure. She was warm and friendly; she knew how to draw people out; she seemed to be genuinely interested in whatever was happening. In a word, the Queen was a thorough professional.

And added to all this was something more: a strong personal magnetism. To those who travelled with her on this tour, her magnetism seemed to have an almost physical quality. The crowds could sense it at once. They responded to her immediately. On one occasion the Minister of Native Affairs, Major Piet van der Byl, who accompanied the family for part of the journey, spoke to her of this magnetism. 'Your Majesty,' he said, 'may I say something, I am not trying to flatter, for that would be gross impertinence, but we all feel a warmth radiating from you. I can't describe it, something intangible. Do you feel that you are giving something out?'

Princess Margaret, Princess Elizabeth, the Queen and the King bid a temporary goodbye to Cape Town as the White Train pulls away from Duncan Dock to start its journey through South Africa.

Her answer was charmingly frank. 'I must admit that at times I feel something flow out of me. It is difficult to describe what I mean. It makes me feel very tired for a moment. Then I seem to get something back from the people – sympathy, good-will – I don't know exactly – and I feel strengthened again, in fact recharged. It's an exchange, I expect; I don't know . . .'

Whatever it was, it ensured the success of the tour. Time and again, by this radiance, the Queen enhanced, or eased, or even at times saved a situation. Without her ever-smiling presence, no occasion would have had the same memorable air. Indeed, if one thing, more than another, came to epitomise the royal tour of South Africa, it was the Queen's brilliant smile. That, and the graceful, fluid, ineffable wave of her white-gloved hand.

4

On Friday 21 February, with Parliament success-fully opened, the royal family began their tour of Southern Africa. Their special train was drawn up on the quayside, beside H.M.S. *Vanguard*. The tensions of the morning's ceremony behind them, the royal family were in a relaxed and cheerful mood as they said goodbye to various dignitaries and officials gathered beside the train. They would he away from Cape Town for over two months.

It took no less than three trains to cope with the needs of the royal party on their journey through the country. The royal family travelled in the 'White Train'. Compared with this latest White Train, the Prince of Wales's train seemed almost run-of-the-mill. It was made up of fourteen superbly appointed

coaches (eight of them built in England and six taken from the Cape Town—Johannesburg 'Blue Train'), all painted ivory and gold, and the whole measuring a third of a mile in length. The hub of the train was a small compartment which served as the King's study. From here the Sovereign could keep in touch not only with Whitehall but with the entire Commonwealth. A sitting-room, a dining-room and four sleeping-compartments, each with its own bathroom, were set aside for the royal family's exclusive use. Their personal staff – private secretaries, ladies-in-waiting and equerries – were accommodated in slightly less spacious quarters. One entire coach, with its own dining-room and kitchen, was reserved for the minister in attendance. This would be a member of the South African cabinet, who was changed from time to time.

The rest of the White Train's passengers were government officials, the tour manager and his staff, the Commissioner of Police and his staff, railway officials, catering managers, electricians and personal servants. Each time the train stopped for the night, a horde of cleaners would wash it down so that it never looked anything less than immaculate.

Half an hour ahead of the White Train steamed the 'Pilot Train'. This carried policemen, lesser railway officials, journalists, photographers, the King's hairdresser and the arranger of flowers in the royal compartments. A special coach carried the administrator of whichever province was being traversed.

These were J. G. Carinus for the Cape Province, Dr S. P. Barnard for the Orange Free State, Mr D. E. Mitchell for Natal and General J. J. Pienaar for the Transvaal. In the Pilot Train also was a post office, a telegraph office and a telephone exchange which could be connected up to the national system as soon as the train stopped.

The third train, travelling several hours behind, was nicknamed the 'Ghost Train'. It carried spare parts and repairing gear for the other two.

With the royal party spending more nights in the train than away from it, suitable nightly stopping-places had to be organised. A water supply, telephone lines and lighting had to be laid on at each place. Sometimes the train was simply shunted onto some side line where the surroundings had been suitably smartened up. In other cases the train would be halted at some espe-cially attractive spot. The royal family were particularly delighted with the Port Elizabeth site; beautified with rock gardens, it gave them a private and unimpeded access to the warm Indian Ocean.

In addition to these three trains, a fleet of over a dozen cars accompanied the royal party through-out the country. As these cars had to be driven from point to point, often over dusty roads, and had always to be waiting sleek and shiny, to pick up the royal party when the train stopped, considerable organisa-tion – and considerable speeds – were necessary. The smoothness with which all this was carried out was one of the minor triumphs of the tour.

The White Train spent the first night (as it would the last) in a lonely vineyard close to the Breede River. On the following day they stopped at Worcester, where the pattern was set for most of the visits to country towns: a reception at the station and a drive through the streets. There was a stop at the Nationalist stronghold of Swellendam and a visit to the largely English-speaking community at George. At Oudtshoorn, famous as the centre of the ostrich-feather industry, the royal family visited an ostrich farm and cut feathers from the birds. Through the vast sheep farms of the Karroo they travelled up to Graaff-Reinet (where the display of flowers in the Town Hall was said to have been dazzling) and down again, through the searing heat, towards the coast.

In a very short time, this gleaming White Train had come to symbolise the royal tour to many South Africans. Some had to be content with a distant view of it puffing across the lonely veld. Others, gathered in a little group at some level-crossing, might catch a fleeting glimpse of a member of the family as the train flashed by. Yet others would be fortunate enough to be at some out-of-the-way siding when the train stopped to take water. In that case, the royal family would invariably alight to greet them.

The siding, lying in the grey-brown folds of the scrubby hills, might be no more than a huddle of sun-baked, corrugated-iron buildings, with the inevitable pepper tree throwing its sparse shade across the cindery platform. A knot of people, from fifty miles away or more, would have gathered to wait, in the burning February sunshine, in the hopes of seeing the royal family. Invariably, the train would be late. Not until hopes had been falsely raised by the passing through of the Pilot Train would the sleek white-and-gold carriages of the royal train come gliding into the station. There would be a short flurry of activity – an alighting of equerries, a few words with the stationmaster, the appearance of yet more officials, the marshalling of the little party of spectators into a line – and then, after a hushed pause, the King would alight.

Slight, sun-tanned, hesitant, wearing a light brown suit, King George VI would wave his hand in answer to the ripple of applause and the one or two self-conscious cheers. He would be followed by the Queen. A consummate actress, she would pause for a moment in the doorway of the carriage, waving a gloved hand in answer to the applause that had suddenly become more spontaneous. Calm, self-possessed, smiling, in a dress and jacket of pale-blue silk and an upswept hat of massed blue and white blossom, she would step down onto the platform. Behind would come the princesses, wearing plain linen dresses and headscarves, their skins aglow in the afternoon light

After a few words to the sweating, serge-suited stationmaster, the Queen would step forward to greet the little crowd. In her light, well-modulated voice and with her head inquiringly tilted, she would ask questions. Had they come far? Where did they live? Oh, yes, Kirkwood, where the oranges grew. Had there been any rain? Yes, it had been very hot. The veld certainly did look very dry. How interesting that the station should be called 'Glenconner'; it reminded one of Scotland.

If she spotted a medal pinned onto some ex-ser-viceman's jacket, she would ask where he had seen service. Here she would turn to involve the King in the conversation. Medals were his passion. If there were children, she would ask their names and their ages. If she noticed anyone who looked old or shy or shabby, she would shake their hands and say, 'I am so glad to meet you. How kind of you to come and see us.'

And so, slowly, down the line they would go, ask-ing, listening, commenting. Occasionally the King would laugh heartily; sometimes the two princesses would join in the conversation. When it was all over and the family was about to board the train, the crowd would break, quaveringly and tentatively, into the two national anthems. And as the train finally pulled out, with the King and Queen framed in one of the Windows, the more robust sound of 'For He's a Jolly Good Fellow' would go drifting after them.

The exhilarated group would break up and begin their long, dusty drive home. But, with luck, they might be granted one more glimpse of the family. Some miles from the siding they would see the White Train drawn up; the royalties were setting off on their daily walk beside the track. And their last view might be of the Queen of England (having changed into sensible shoes) striding across the desolate veld in that towering, flowery, sumptuous hat.

On the mind of at least one sixteen-year-old boy, such an afternoon's encounter was to leave an indelible impression.

5

The White Train arrived in Port Elizabeth on 26 February. The royal family particularly enjoyed their two-day stay in this bustling seaport with its strongly British flavour. They were given a tremendous welcome by two gatherings of schoolchildren, one white and one black; they drove through the streets of the great African township, New Brighton; they gave up some of their free time to visit the neighbouring town of Uitenhage; fascinated, they watched the writhings of the deadly reptiles in the city's famous Snake Park; there was the inevitable parade of ex-servicemen and the no less inevitable garden party. And, whenever they could, the family took advantage of the waves that crashed so invitingly along the stretch of beach beside their train. Even the Queen was seen to paddle.

Leaving the train at Alicedale, the party drove to Grahamstown. Their reception in this charming university city was quite different from that in the university town of Stellenbosch: the citizens of Grahamstown, so conscious of their British heritage, were gratifyingly enthusiastic. On the following day they again left the train, this time at Alice, to visit the great African educational centre of Lovedale.

The royal family was deeply moved by the singing of a choir of over five-thousand students; 'Their soft and limpid harmonies, rising unaccompanied in the sunshine of an absolutely still morning, while big and gaudy butterflies flitted in and out among the royal party on the platform, will long be remembered. . . .' wrote one of the visitors.

More singing greeted them at every station on the way to East London and, as they neared the port, hundreds upon hundreds of cars kept pace with the train on the road that ran beside the track. In East London, the heiress presumptive, Princess Elizabeth, performed her first solo duty: she opened a new graving dock. In spite of the wind which tugged at her hat, her skirt and her notes, she acquitted herself charmingly. Her father's eyes were said to have filled with tears as, in the White Train, he listened to a broadcast of her speech.

At King William's Town there was a great tribal gathering ('By *command* of His Majesty the King,' was the King's urgently whispered correction to the Chief Native Commissioner, who had said 'On behalf of His Majesty the King' as he presented medals to various chiefs) and then the party boarded the train to enter the Transkei, one of the main African Reserves.

The Minister in Attendance, Major Piet van der Byl, and his elegant wife Joy had been invited to dine with the royal family in their private dining-saloon the night the train entered the Transkei. Halfway through the meal the train stopped.

'Heavens,' exclaimed the King, 'we haven't got to get out again, have we?'

'No, Sir, this is the Kei Bridge,' explained Van der Byl. 'We are now in the Transkei – we are no longer entirely under the Common Law. From here on you rule, Sir, by proclamation as issued by your Minister of Native Affairs.'

As Van der Byl himself was Minister of Native Affairs, the King immediately began to tease him. 'Well, let's issue some – advise me what I should proclaim!' he demanded. Bizarre proclamations and bannings were suggested and, as the royal train went racing on through the night, the banter became more and more animated.

Watched by Mrs Sturrock, Princess Elizabeth receives a gift of diamonds from F.C. Sturrock (Minister of Railways and Harbours) after opening the new graving-dock in East London. Behind, from left, stand Mrs Joy van der Byl, Harry Lawrence, Lady Margaret Egerton (lady-in-waiting to the Princess), Major Piet van der Byl, Mrs Jean Lawrence (partly obscured) and, in white hat on right, Mrs J.G. Carinus.

*The royal party watches the reptiles in Port
Elizabeth's famous Snake Park.*

These frothy exchanges concealed a core of seri-
ousness. They were indeed in a territory where the
Sovereign could issue proclamations. In theory the
King, and not the South African administration, was
the ultimate master of the fates of these millions of
tribal Africans. On 5 March, amid the rolling hills
outside the Transkeian capital of Umtata, some tens
of thousands of Xhosa were gathered to greet this
supreme chief. For the occasion, the King wore his
white uniform of an Admiral of the Fleet, with the
blue Garter ribbon across his chest and a gold-hilted
sword by his side. Yet, despite the fact that the rest
of his staff were inconspicuously dressed, in ordinary
suits, there was a feeling that the monarch did not

look impressive enough. The Africans had obviously expected to see someone more spectacularly dressed. The same complaint was to be heard at all the *indabas* during the tour.

But a lesson had been learned. Princess Elizabeth, as Queen Elizabeth II, would always appear before such African subjects as remained in the Commonwealth in full evening dress and flashing tiara.

Chief Moshesh, at the close of his address to the King, gave the traditional cry of '*Pula! Pula!* – Rain! Rain!' For in a land where rain is regarded as a blessing, the visit of a great chief is believed to be followed by rain. And so it was. An hour after the royal party left, the clouds began to pile up. By nightfall it was raining.

After several more station stops and visits to Queenstown and Aliwal North (where the mayor insisted that the King sit on the mayoral chair because a silver plate had already been engraved to that effect) the White Train crossed the Orange River. Hitherto, with one or two exceptions, the royal family had passed through areas of the country which were generally sympathetic towards the monarchy. Now, on crossing into the Orange Free State, they were entering one of the great republican strongholds.

6

It started badly. At a quarter to eleven at night, soon after the White Train first entered the Free State, it suddenly stopped. Officials, peering out into the rain-lashed darkness, were astonished to see a crowd of people collected at a little station. This was not a scheduled stop. The local stationmaster had obviously decided to pull down the signals and halt the train. Here was a dilemma. The royal family had already retired; the train was running very late and the guard was all for giving the signal to start up immediately; and a party of people, braving the sneers of their Nationalist neighbours, had stood for hours in the rain in the hope of seeing the King. It would not have mattered so much anywhere else, but here, at the start of the Free State tour, the non-appearance of the King could be very damaging.

And it seemed as though he was not going to appear. The distraught Piet van der Byl, placating the disappointed local mayor on one hand and the impatient guard of the train on the other, begged an equerry to coax the King to come out. At first, there was no sign of him. Only after a nerve-racking delay did he appear. The King, who could be short-tempered on occasion, was in a temper now. 'Why was I not warned?' he asked angrily. Van der Byl had just explained the situation when the Queen suddenly appeared in the doorway. 'I heaved a sigh of relief,' he says. 'A smile, a wave of her hand and the crowd would melt.'

And so it proved to be. Down onto the muddy platform they went – the King, the Queen and the princesses, all in evening dress – to talk to the crowd. The Queen, appreciating the situation, 'walked more slowly, stopped more frequently and talked longer than usual. Sometimes the King would be ten yards ahead and had to wait. . . .' writes Van der Byl. 'Her Majesty, though very tired after a long day, did it wholeheartedly. I had never been so grateful to anyone in my life.'

If the reception in Bloemfontein was a little less vociferous than in some other cities, it was no less courteous. The Nationalist mayor, J.G.Bernade, welcomed the royal guests with the utmost cordiality. With this dignified city being both the capital of the Free State and the judicial capital of the Union of South Africa, things took on a slightly more formal flavour. There was a reception in the old republican Raadsaal and, for the first time since leaving Cape Town, the royal family slept away from the White Train, at a Government House. For the rest, there were the customary functions: the tea party in the City Hall, the gathering of schoolchildren, the garden party and the civic ball. A day was spent in the Free State Game Reserve. The party flew there in two Vikings of the King's Flight (it was the first time that Princess Margaret had ever flown) and the family enjoyed a *braaivleis* under the thorn trees. In the Bloemfontein Cathedral on Sunday 9 March, the King was so impressed by a special prayer offered up for the British people, then suffering that particularly cruel winter, that he asked for a copy of it.

'The thoughts of the people on the constitutional question', noted one British journalist at the end of

the Bloemfontein visit, 'may or may not show a modifi-
cation in the coming years, when the long-term effects
of the royal visit come to be estimated; but on the personal side the feelings f friendship between the Royal
Family and their South African subjects had been as
well established in Bloemfontein as in cities where
acceptance of the monarchical idea is undisputed.'

*The two princesses set out for a ride across the Free
State veld before breakfast one morning.*

Visits to Kroonstad, Bethlehem and Ladybrand completed the journey through the vast, ochre-coloured grasslands of the Free State. The atmosphere in all three was highly relaxed: there was a tea party in one, a flower show in the other, and an open air concert in the third. The Queen was particularly struck by the good manners of the crowds. 'They do not push themselves forward nor were they effusive, but on the other hand, when talked to, they were perfectly natural and quiet.' They reminded her, she said, of Scottish people.

Temporarily leaving the Union and entering British territory, the visitors quit their train to drive along a hastily tarred road into Maseru, the capital of Basutoland. For days, horsemen from all over this small, mountainous state had been jogging towards the little capital, where a great national assembly, a *Pitso*, was to be held. It took place on 12 March – a colourful, exuberant, dust-clouded, strangely moving occasion, at which the King invested various Basuto soldiers and civilians A more sedate investiture, for the white community, was held during a garden party at the Residency that afternoon. Basutoland was still a Crown Colony, and over all the proceedings fluttered the red, white and blue of the Union Jack.

Re-entering the Free State, the royal party stopped briefly at Harrismith and then their train wound down through the spectacular Drakensberg Mountains into the garden province of Natal. Here Smuts, who had tactfully avoided appearing with the royal family in the Orange Free State, rejoined them and accompanied them to Ladysmith. At the parade of ex-servicemen at the Ladysmith Oval, Smuts was cheered almost as warmly as the King.

There followed, after Ladysmith, a much-needed four-day holiday. The party drove to the Natal National Park and there, among its awe-inspiring mountain scenery, they gave themselves over to the simple delights of walking, climbing, bathing and fishing. With the King in shorts, the princesses in cotton dresses and even the Queen in an unadorned straw hat, the family could forget, for a while, the rigours and the responsibilities of their journey.

7

Those who came to know the royal family during these weeks of travel were struck by the harmonious relationship between them. They were obviously an extraordinarily happy family. A great deal of this was due to Queen Elizabeth's tactful and good-natured personality; she knew exactly how to handle her more highly-strung husband and how to encourage her still immature daughters.

The girls adored their parents. To them the King and Queen were 'Pop' and 'Mummy'; Princess Margaret always referred to her sister as 'Lilibet'. They all took a great interest and pride in each other's appearance. 'Come and look at Mummy's jewels and orders,' the princesses would say when their parents were dressed for a ball, and the King and Queen would take pleasure in discussing their various jewels and decorations. Both the King and Princess Elizabeth were particularly interested in medals and orders. Whenever there was a pause before some official function, the four of them would gather in a little group, adjusting each other's jewellery or rearranging each other's clothes. When they were being driven for long distances across the veld, they would amuse themselves by singing round songs.

They were full of family jokes. And this tour, of course, provided them with more. At one ball a handsome, celebrated but painfully inarticulate Springbok rugby player had been commandeered to partner Princess Elizabeth; after a frantic casting about for something to say, he suddenly blurted out, 'I saw your Mom and Dad in town today.'

But their favourite standing joke on the tour was the question asked of each other whenever they were in gala dress: 'Is this a special occasion?' It appears that during the King's tour of Canada before the war, he once noticed that a local mayor was not wearing a mayoral chain. The King, planning to present him with one, asked him whether or not he had a chain.

'Oh, yes, Sir,' answered the mayor. 'I have.'

'But I notice you are not wearing it,' said the King.

'Oh,' explained the mayor, 'but I only wear it on special occasions.'

8

In Natal the royal visitors were brought face to face with yet another facet of South Africa's racial dilemma.

By now the Indian population of the province almost equalled that of the white people. For several years the Natal Indian Congress had been clamouring for equal rights with the Europeans, while the Europeans, with the cry that 'white civilisation' must be saved in Natal, were just as vehement in resisting the granting of any such rights. Smuts's attempt to provide a compromise solution (by introducing the Asiatic Representation and Land Tenure Bill) pleased no one and brought him into open conflict with India. Indeed, a few weeks before the start of the royal tour, the United Nations formally censured South Africa for its treatment of its Indian subjects.

With the King-Emperor about to grant independence to India, the Natal Indian Congress saw no reason why they should welcome this same King-Emperor in whose name rights were being withheld from them. They therefore decided to boycott the visit. Let the ultra-royalist, loyal-hearted, Union-Jack-waving white Natalians, who so eagerly embraced everything British except the British liberal tradition, have the field to themselves.

But, human nature being what it is, the boycott was not a success. Everywhere in Natal the royal visitors were met with, and charmed by, the grace and dignity and courtesy of the Indian women in their colourful saris. In Pietermaritzburg, where the family arrived on 18 March, the entertainment provided by the Indian community eclipsed all others. The morning had seen the usual ceremonies: the reception at the station, the addresses of welcome in the City Hall by the Administrator and the Mayor (it was a woman mayor in this case, Mrs W.A.D. Russell), the drive through the clamorous, decorated streets and the rally of schoolchildren. Later, there would be a garden party. But in the afternoon, at an assembly of the Indian community, fifty girls, all in brilliant saris, performed their fluid and stately dances for the royal guests. It gave the party one of their most vivid memories of the tour.

On the balcony of Pietermaritzburg's flamboyant City Hall and facing an uncompromising-looking row of mounted policemen, King George VI replies to the city's address of welcome.

*At Estcourt, Natal, the Queen stops to talk to
a gathering of cubs and brownies*

*The King and Queen speaking to members of
the Indian community in Durban.*

*The Queen speaks to a uniformed servicewoman at
a garden party in Mitchell Park, Durban.*

The following day's dancing proved to be infinitely more energetic. The royal party drove through the green hills of Zululand to Eshowe for a Zulu *indaba*. As the King, in his white uniform, mounted the dais, the great cry of '*Bayete! Bayete! Bayete!*' went up from the tens of thousands of Zulu gathered there. Chief Albert Luthuli, a future Nobel Prize winner, who was to suffer banning at the hands of the Nationalist government, pronounced the colourful speech of welcome. The gentle King must have been somewhat startled to find himself compared to an 'elephant whose tread shakes the earth' and a 'lion whose roaring causes all the rest of creation to be respectfully silent'.

The customary presentation of medals was followed by a series of chanting, earth-shaking, knob-kerrie-waving, shield-thumping, plume-tossing and frankly frightening war dances. 'It is almost menacing when they work themselves up like that,' murmured the Queen as yet another wave of warriors dashed up towards the dais.

On Thursday 20 March the royal family drove into Durban. They were given, of course, a stupendous welcome, the most enthusiastic of the tour. For four days, in the most enervating weather they had yet encountered, they carried out a full programme of engagements. They were officially welcomed on a dais outside Durban's flamboyantly Edwardian City Hall by another of those accomplished mayoral couples, Rupert and Clare Ellis Brown. In the square below, the King swung open the Gate of Rememberance, added to the cenotaph in memory of the dead of the Second World War. Through packed streets they drove to King's House, the elegant hilltop residence which was at last fulfilling the purpose for which it had been built. In the evening there was a crowded ball at the City Hall. The sight of the Queen in shimmering satin, all sparkling with jewels, as she appeared on the dais outside the hall, so astonished the crowd that there was a hush until she raised her hand in greeting.

At the end of the ball, with the royal family safely seen off, the relieved and delighted mayoral couple fell into each other's arms and embraced.

A great rally of schoolchildren (at which 'Land of Hope and Glory' was bellowed out), a garden party in Mitchell Park, another African *indaba,* a reception by the Indian community at Currie's Fountain, a parade of ex-servicemen (at which the royal family stood for almost an hour in torrid heat) and a visit to the races, which is said to have ended – after the royal party had left – in the punters and judges almost coming to blows, completed their Durban programme.

After a visit to Vryheid in northern Natal, the royal party crossed into the Transvaal.

On the lawns beneath the Union Buildings, Pretoria, the Queen exercises her considerable charm on a gathering of oudstryders.

193

9

Before reaching one of the great climaxes of the tour – the stay in the administrative capital of Pretoria with visits to the huge city of Johannesburg – the royal family spent a few days in the Eastern Transvaal.

Again, under the rippling Union Jack and in a beautiful mountain territory – the Crown Colony of Swaziland – the King attended a tumultuous African *indaba* and a sedate European garden party. Back in the Union, at Ermelo, as an echo of the days when his brother, the Prince of Wales, toured South Africa, the King was escorted into town by a Boer commando. At Standerton, to welcome him on the steps of the Magistrate's Court, was another Boer War veteran, Field-Marshal Smuts. This was the centre of the Prime Minister's parliamentary constituency. At an open-air luncheon that day, the party was entertained by a display of *volkspele*: they declared themselves enchanted. A day was spent in the famous Kruger National Park, with the King himself driving the Queen through this paradise of wild life.

On 29 March the royal visitors made their official entry into the very heart of Afrikanerdom – Pretoria.

Two great structures dominated and, in a way, fought for the soul of this elegant city. On one hill rose that massive shrine of Afrikaner republicanism, the still unfinished Voortrekker Monument; on another lay that symbol of Boer-British reconciliation, the serene and gracefully sprawling Union Buildings.

Reconciliation was of course to be the keynote of the royalties' visit to Pretoria. Their official welcome took place in the centre of the old republican capital, Church Square, where, on a dais facing the top-hatted statue of President Kruger, they were received by the Mayor, Mr D.P. van Heerden. On the sweeping lawns below the Union Buildings they moved amongst a great gathering of *oudstryders* – grey-bearded veterans of the Anglo-Boer War, on whom the Queen exercised all her charm. At a state banquet in the City Hall, the King made a particularly moving speech during which he paid tribute to the traditions of the Afrikaner people. On the Sunday, the family attended morning service in the Dutch Reformed Church. (The Anglican Princess Margaret, rising to her feet at some point in the service, was tugged back into her seat by her more knowing Scots mother.)

But there were other, more routine engagements. In a drizzle, the family attended a garden party; thirty thousand white schoolchildren cheered to their hearts' content at Loftus Versfeld grounds; in a contrasting silence they drove through a gathering of overawed black children; the King presented colours at a great military parade at Voortrekkerhoogte (as the name of Lord Roberts was anathema to General Hertzog, his government had changed the name of Roberts Heights to Voortrekkerhoogte); the family flew to Pietersburg in the northern Transvaal, where they attended another huge *indaba*, at which the

singing – unaccompanied, deep-throated, plaintive –
was particularly moving.

One afternoon they paid a visit to 'Doornkloof',
Smuts's unpretentious corrugated-iron farmhouse,
where they were entertained to tea by his equally
unpretentious but by no means unintelligent wife,
the famous 'Ouma' Smuts. Bespectacled, frizzy-
haired, and in a dark dress, the honest-to-goodness
Ouma, who played very little part in her husband's
public life, sat on the stoep with the King and Queen
of England.

*At Turffontein racecourse, Johannesburg, the royal fam-
ily make their way through the spectators.*

All in all, the royal family spent eight nights in
Government House, Pretoria. It was their longest
time away from the White Train, and the bracing,
autumnal highveld air made their stay very pleasant.
During this period the royalties paid three visits – two
scheduled and one unscheduled – to Johannesburg
and the Reef.

There was some dissatisfaction at the fact that only two days had been allotted to what was far and away the largest, wealthiest and most ebullient city in South Africa. But if there was, none of it was allowed to show. As the royal procession came driving from the outskirts into the densely packed heart of this extraordinary city, they were given a rapturous welcome. There seemed to be a million people, not only in the streets but hanging from every window and balcony of the soaring blocks of buildings. The usual reception in the City Hall was followed by the most exhausting two days of the tour. The King unveiled a new inscription on the cenotaph; he reviewed a parade of ex-servicemen; he opened the Rand Agricultural Show; there was a luncheon in the City Hall; a visit to Turffontein racecourse to see the running of the King's Cup; a state banquet in the City Hall; and a dance for the princesses at which the King and Queen looked in for an hour.

On the second day the royal family toured the straggling towns of the East and West Rand. In open cars, in blazing sunshine and drifting dust, they drove for hours on end along the Reef, smiling, waving, apparently inexhaustible. The chief break was hardly more relaxing: it was another formal luncheon in the Johannesburg City Hall. And they had to be every bit as alert as they looked, for at one moment during the day's interminable drive, an African suddenly charged towards the slow-moving royal car. Her smile undimmed, the Queen deftly lowered her sunshade so as to protect the King from what might well have been an attack. But the over-excited man had been bent, not on assassination, but on presenting Princess Elizabeth with a ten-shilling note.

Appreciating that not enough of their time had been devoted to this pulsating city, the royal family gave up a free day – 5 April – to pay it another visit. They attended two rallies of schoolchildren. In helmets and white coats they went down a gold mine. They paid a visit to the Baragwanath Military Hospital. Here, to the despair of the more time-conscious authorities, the Queen lingered by each bed, bringing what comfort she could. 'It is one long grind of unselfish labour,' wrote an admiring cabinet minister in attendance, 'with never a real break from work and duty, never a let-up. Work, work and again work, under an almost unbelievable physical and psychological strain.'

The sun was already setting when they left Johannesburg. In that short-lived, marvellous high-veld dusk, the royal party drove back to Pretoria.

10

One of the ways in which this 1947 tour differed from the Prince of Wales's tour two decades before was that some notice was taken of the urban Africans; not much, but some.

Although the white population might like to pretend otherwise, the black proletariat had by now become a permanent and essential part of city life.

Huge black townships, some uniform and soulless, some ramshackle and vibrant, now sprawled on the fringes of every major city. Often the black populations equalled or outstripped the white; to believe that they were anything other than permanent city-dwellers was futile. Yet their status remained undefined. Without rights of franchise or tenure, yet no longer tribal, they inhabited a sort of never-never-land.

But at least some acknowledgement was paid to their existence this time. In each of the large cities of the country, the royal family was allowed some contact with the African population. Often it would mean nothing more than a drive through the streets of the townships; sometimes the visitors would attend an ill-defined assembly, neither tribal nor urban; there were gatherings of scrubbed and blazered schoolchildren; in Johannesburg the royalties visited Africans in the mine compounds. They were always enthusiastically greeted. If the visitors did not believe that quite everything in the garden was rosy, they perhaps imagined that things would improve in time. In any case, there was nothing that they could do about it except to treat everyone with equal charm and courtesy. It was a long time since Britain, and a much longer time still since the Sovereign had had any say in South African affairs.

All this made the atmosphere during the next eleven days, from 7 to 17 April, rather different. For the royal family spent that time in Southern Rhodesia and Bechuanaland. Southern Rhodesia was, in most respects, a self-governing dominion, and

Bechuanaland was still a British protectorate, but both were multiracial territories. In theory, at any rate, the black man was equal to the white.

One could notice the difference from the start. In the Salisbury crowd (the family had flown the six hundred miles from Pretoria to Salisbury) black and white were 'more closely interspersed than was usual in the Union'. The King, on 7 April, opened the Southern Rhodesian Parliament, to which members were elected by both Europeans and Africans. The garden party was open to all races. Princess Elizabeth was given an early birthday present (a flame-lily brooch in platinum and diamonds) by six children – two European, one Coloured, one Indian and two African – representing the various race groups in the country. The guides and brownies, inspected by the two princesses, were black and white.

But with tribalism, both European and African, being far from dead, there were some more familiar occasions: a colourful *indaba* on the Salisbury racecourse, an inspection of some fifty survivors of the original Pioneer Column which had opened up Rhodesia to white settlement in 1890, and a reception given by the Governor, Sir John Kennedy, at Government House for about a thousand 'leading members of the European community'.

From Salisbury, the family again boarded the White Train (which had been brought up during their stay in Pretoria) and, after stopping at various country towns – Hartley, Gatooma, Que Que – arrived at the Victoria

Falls on 11 April. Here they stayed for three days at the Victoria Falls Hotel. The short stay was something of a holiday. The only official engagement was a visit across the Zambezi by launch to Livingstone in Northern Rhodesia. For the rest of the time the family could see their fill of that churning, awe-inspiring and endlessly fascinating fall of water. It was then that the King cabled the two daughters of Princess Christian, to say that he had named two islands after them.

By 14 April the visitors were in Bulawayo. The highlight of this stay was the obligatory visit to 'World's View', that bald, sombre, boulder-strewn hilltop on which the body of Cecil John Rhodes lay buried. The ascent was steep and slippery and proved too much for the Queen's high heels. So Princess Elizabeth lent her mother her own, flat, shoes and finished the climb in stockinged feet. The future Queen of England stood gazing at the simple gravestone of the man whose vision had been largely responsible for bringing the whole of Southern Africa under the sway of the British Crown. In less than twenty years, and during her reign, the greater part of the vast sub-continent would have broken away.

After the usual garden party, the meeting with the survivors of the Pioneer Column, and the Government House reception, the royal family left Bulawayo on the White Train for the long return journey to Cape Town. Through Bechuanaland, along the edge of the great Kalahari desert, they travelled. For hour after hour the train chugged through the flat, featureless, sunburnt countryside, stopping finally at Lobatsi, near the border with the Union. Here there was a brief round of ceremonies. Even in this remote and arid outpost, the influence of imperial Britain had left its mark. There were uniformed girl guides, medalled ex-servicemen, and two African chiefs, one in the scarlet of the Dragoon Guards, the other in the blue of the Royal Horse Guards, and both resplendent in silver helmets, horsehair, gold braid, brass buttons and ceremonial swords.

Beside them, the King-Emperor looked as nothing.

11

On 17 April the White Train re-entered the Union just before Mafeking. There remained a thousand-mile journey, most of it across a vast, open landscape, before they again reached Cape Town.

At the Victoria Falls.

With the ascent up 'World's View', Rhodesia, too steep for the Queen's high heels, Princess Elizabeth lent her shoes to her mother and finished the climb in stockinged feet.

The King inspects an African guard of honour during the short stop at Lobatsi in Bechuanaland.

In the once famous siege town of Mafeking, their reception was so high-spirited that at least one member of the party suspected that some of the townsfolk must be drunk. In that other no less famous siege town, Kimberley, which they reached the following day, the atmosphere was more dignified. The famous Kimberley Club was put at the family's disposal (the Queen left one of her rings on the wash-hand basin and it had to be sent on), and it was here that they attended a luncheon. There was a garden reception, a parade of ex-servicemen and a rally of schoolchildren. To show the visitors over the De Beers buildings and the celebrated 'Big Hole' was the Chairman of the company, Sir Ernest Oppenheimer, accompanied by his son Harry and Harry's soignée wife Bridget Little Mary Oppenheimer presented each of the princesses with a magnificent diamond, and when in all innocence Princess Margaret asked, 'And what about Mummy's?', Sir Ernest presented the Queen with a diamond from his own collection. This, says one chronicler, 'was graciously received by the Queen'.

After a short stop at Beaufort West in the heart of the Great Karroo, the White Train came gliding into the very vineyard, near the Breede River, in which it had rested on the first night of its journey. This would be the last stop of the tour. The royal family took leave of their fellow passengers; to each they presented signed portraits or commemorative medallions. On the following morning – Sunday 20 April – the train arrived on the quayside at Cape Town, from where it had set off two months before. The royal family were met by a host of dignitaries, headed by the Governor-General.

To the Mayoress of Cape Town, Mrs Miriam Bloomberg, the Queen admitted that it felt like coming home.

12

On Monday 21 April Princess Elizabeth came of age.

During the course of the South African tour, the future Queen Elizabeth II had gradually developed into a personality in her own right. The speculation on whether or not she was to become engaged to Lieutenant Philip Mountbatten had given her a certain intriguing quality from the start; the public would have been more intrigued still had they known that she often telephoned him from the White Train during the night stops. (The seeds of yet another royal romance were being sown on this tour as well, for travelling with the family as one of the King's equerries was the handsome Peter Townsend. His love affair with Princess Margaret was to be one of the great royal dramas of the 1950s.)

As the tour progressed, so Princess Elizabeth began to reveal herself as an individual of considerable presence and ability. Not for many years, if ever, would she be able to match her mother's aplomb but, left to herself, she behaved with grace and dignity. In private, and at ease, she could be charming.

Her birthday saw her on her own, and at her best. In a dress and hat of pale *café au lait*, she took the salute at a march-past of troops at Young's Field aerodrome. Present on this important ceremonial occasion were the Prime Minister, the Cabinet and the entire Diplomatic Corps. In the afternoon she attended an enthusiastic youth rally at the Rosebank Showgrounds. That night Cape Town was *en fête*. There was a dazzling display of fireworks; a ball at the City Hall, at which the Princess, in white tulle sparkling with silver, was presented with a birthday gift by the Mayor; and another ball in the white-and-gold ballroom of Government House. Here the delighted Princess was presented with a magnificent necklace, made up of twenty-one flashing diamonds.

Earlier that evening the Princess had broadcast a special twenty-first birthday message to the Commonwealth. To many it seemed fitting that this important speech, by the heir presumptive to the throne, should be made in one of the Commonwealth countries; it seemed to underline the fact that the royal family belonged as much to South Africa, or any other member of the Commonwealth, as it did to Great Britain. It was as the future Queen of South Africa – or Australia or Canada – that Princess Elizabeth now addressed herself to her future subjects.

Queen Elizabeth, radiant in oyster satin and glittering with jewels.

Having spoken, first, of South Africa, where she felt so much at home, she asked all the nations of the British Commonwealth to witness what she called her 'solemn act of dedication'.

'I should like', she said in that still-girlish voice, 'to make that dedication now. It is very simple. I declare before you all that my whole life, whether it be long or short, shall be devoted to your service and the service of our great Imperial Commonwealth to which we all belong. But I shall not have strength to carry out this resolution unless you join in it with me, as I now invite you to do; I know that your support will be unfailingly given. God help me to make good my vow and God bless all of you who are willing to share in it.'

13

But not everyone was willing to help Princess Elizabeth make good her vow of dedication to the 'great Imperial Commonwealth'.

Before the tour started, General Kemp, a leading Nationalist, had pronounced on the forthcoming royal visit. 'The position of the Afrikaner and Republican is clear,' he said. 'Those of us who took part in the South African War, or whose forebears took part, and who have since striven and are striving still for a Republic in South Africa, and other pro-Republicans, cannot take part in a festivity which will strengthen the monarchy in the Union.'

And when, in the course of the tour, the royal family visited Johannesburg, the editor of *Die Transvaler,*

H. F. Verwoerd (destined to become the most uncompromising exponent of *apartheid*), refused to mention their arrival. There had been a spate of burglaries, his newspaper reported on the day after the visit, because the city's police had been obliged to give all their attention to the visitors.

Deeply conscious of this hostility, the royal family had done what they could to combat it. Often, by their charm and their simplicity and their frankness, they seemed to be melting the antagonism. One old Nationalist, who had fought not only in the Anglo-Boer War but in the 1914 rebellion against the Botha administration, was so impressed by his talk with the King that he tore off his ornamental leather belt (which the King had admired) and, running alongside the moving White Train, passed it up to one of the equerries, shouting, 'Here, give it to him!' To another *oudstryder,* who had told her that he could never forgive the British for fighting against the Boers, the Queen deftly admitted that, as a Scot, she understood his attitude perfectly.

In Bloemfontein, the King paid a visit to the aged widow of the last President of the Free State; 'a wonderful old lady' reported the Queen to Queen Mary. And in Cape Town the King returned President Kruger's Bible, taken by the British during the Anglo-Boer War, with the request that it be handed back to his family. Be it *jukskei* or *volkspele* or *melktert* or *boerewors* or *boerebeskuit* or *boeremusiek* or 'Sarie Marais' played *ad nauseam,* the royalties expressed nothing but appreciation. Few speeches ended without a tentative line of Afrikaans or a badly pronounced '*tot siens*'.

In the course of the last few days in Cape Town, the royalties made one final effort. They had a private meeting with the leader of the National Party, Dr D. F. Malan. Accompanied by his wife the spirited Maria Malan, the leader of the Opposition spent a little while with the King and Queen. The talk was confined to pleasantries. 'As was only right,' Malan afterwards said, 'nothing was discussed that had any political meaning. Our conversation was quite informal and friendly.' After a while, the two princesses were called into the room. They all parted on the most amicable of terms. It had not been, it could not have been, much; but it was something.

14

There were not many days left. On 22 April, while the King, in relaxed and merry mood, presided over a meeting of the Executive Council, the Queen was having the honorary degree of Doctor of Laws conferred upon her by the University of Cape Town. That afternoon, while their parents paid a private visit to the farm 'Vergelegen' near Somerset West, the princesses went for a flip over the Peninsula in one of the Vikings of the King's Flight. In the City Hall that night, the Queen sat through an interminable concert with every sign of apparent employment. The King, wisely, stayed home.

The royal party coming down in the cable car from the top of Table Mountain. Behind the King and Queen stands Jannie Hofmeyr.

The following morning the royal visitor: took the cableway up Table Mountain. To meet them at the top was the seventy-six-year-old Field Marshal Smuts, who had climbed up the mountain. From the sunlit but chilly summit, they enjoyed a breathtaking view of the Peninsula. 'I could see a glow of enthusiasm, surprise and wonder on the faces of the royal family,' claimed Smuts. 'I am sure they went back with the feeling that Table Mountain was the grandest in the world.'

With a feather from the Queen's elaborate hat stuck into his own simple panama, Smuts led them for a brisk walk along the summit. The Queen, remembering her struggle up 'World's View' in Rhodesia, had brought a change of shoes this time.

Smuts, not only on the summit of Table Mountain but throughout the royal tour, was in his element. While his lieutenant, J. H. Hofmeyr, had been left, as he put it, 'to mind the Parliamentary baby', Smuts appeared time and time again beside the royal family. There were very few photographs of the tour in which he did not appear. There were some who considered this excessive royal hobnobbing not only unctuous but unwise. 'At his age', Hofmeyr's sharp-tongued old mother would say, 'he ought to know better.' But Smuts was irresistibly attracted to the institution of monarchy, and for the Queen in particular he had the highest admiration. 'Beside her, my boy,' he once said to a companion, 'we are all small potatoes.'

Down again from the mountain, the two uniformed princesses attended a guide and scout rally. There was a small informal party among the autumn splendour of the Administrator's garden at Leeuwenhof and yet another parade of ex-servicemen, at which the Queen, having come on directly from the garden party, appeared in a long dress and furs. With the King becoming increasingly agitated at the sluggishness with which the parade seemed to be getting under way, the Queen was seen to be gently stroking his arm in an effort to soothe him.

Finally, on the last day – 24 April – there was a farewell luncheon at the City Hall. It was an emotional occasion, suffused with melancholy. 'All the various sections of your people, of all races and colours,' said Smuts in his speech to the King, 'have been thrilled by meeting with the Royal Family, and their lives have been enriched by this experience of human contact on the highest level. Your visit has been a blessing to us, at a time calling specially for a royal blessing.'

In his speech of reply, the King expressed the hope that South Africans would build up 'a great country with a high and honoured place, not only in Africa, but also among the nations of the world.' May it advance, he said, 'from strength to strength, in justice and righteousness, and in happiness to all its people'.

When, quite unexpectedly, the Queen rose to say a few words, there was a ripple of excitement. Speaking with obvious emotion, the Queen offered her personal thanks to the women and children of South Africa.

Through crowded streets, between the packed stands on the foreshore and down onto the quayside drove the royal visitors. With the great grey bulk of H.M.S. *Vanguard* as a background, goodbyes were said to the various officials, ministers, the Prime Minister and the Governor-General and Mrs Brand Van Zyl. When the two anthems had crashed out for the final time, the four familiar figures stepped onto the gangplank and disappeared into the ship. A few minutes later they re-emerged on the platform above the forward gun turret.

Slowly, smoothly, the *Vanguard* began to move away from the quay. As the family, becoming smaller and smaller, stood waving their last farewells to the crowds, a selection of those plaintive, heart-rending songs floated across the churning waters, 'God be with you till we meet again', 'Will ye no' come back again?' and finally, most poignant of all, 'Auld Lang Syne'.

H.M.S. *Vanguard* swung round and, slipping out of the harbour mouth, made for the open sea.

15

'Never', said Smuts in his speech on the occasion of that last luncheon, 'in the history of this, your South African dominion, has there been such a wave of personal and national emotion as your visit has stirred

among us. The immediate experience has been tremendous, and its after-effects will endure. . . .'

The immediate experience might well have
been tremendous but the after-effects can hardly be
said to have endured. In just over a year after the
royal visit, South Africa went to the polls. Although
Smuts's United Party won more votes, the National
Party, allied to the Afrikaner Party, won more seats.
Malan's victory was narrow but the swing towards him
had been immense. It had obviously needed a great
deal more than royal smiles to offset racial fears and
domestic discontent.

For the moment, however, the new Nationalist
government was prepared to put the republican issue
in cold storage. King George VI remained Head of
State, and his death early in 1952 was mourned as the
death of South Africa's Sovereign. Indeed, the King,
the Queen and Princess Margaret, at the invitation
of Dr Malan, had been due to pay another visit to
South Africa that year, to allow the King to recuper-
ate from an illness. Dr and Mrs Malan attended the
coronation of Queen Elizabeth II, and South Africa's
Governor-General, although a Nationalist, continued
to represent the Crown

But if the republican issue had been temporarily
shelved, the *apartheid* policies of the new government
were being implemented with all possible determination. Inevitably, this led to trouble within the
Commonwealth. A system based on racial discrimina-
tion could hardly be countenanced in a multiracial

organisation, many of whose members were newly independent African states.

Once the Nationalist government felt itself firmly enough established (its majority had increased with each election), it could again turn its attention to the emotive issue of a republic. On 5 October 1960 a referendum, in which only the white electorate voted, was held on the issue. A four-percent majority voted in favour of a republic. Five months later, at the Commonwealth Prime Ministers' Conference, the South African Prime Minister, Dr Verwoerd, applied for continued membership of the Commonwealth in event of South Africa becoming a republic. Not unnaturally, the conference was a stormy one, with South Africa's abhorrent racial policy the chief topic of discussion. Dr Verwoerd felt compelled to withdraw his application, and return home.

On 31 May 1961, South Africa became a republic and ceased to be a member of the Commonwealth. The century-and-a-half-long link with Britain, symbolised by the Crown, was finally broken. A president replaced Queen Elizabeth II as the South African Head of State.

EPILOGUE

COULD THE BREAK BETWEEN SOUTH AFRICA AND THE crown have been avoided? Not by 1960, by then it had become almost inevitable. Only if, somewhere along the line, South Africa had taken a different racial path could the rupture with the Commonwealth have been avoided. But, paradoxically, with the final uniting of the entire country under the British Crown in 1910, the opportunity of remaining under that Crown was lost. The price of Boer-British co-operation was the loss, in the years that followed, of any possibility of black-white co-operation. At the time of Union, the former was considered more important. It was in their efforts to keep white South Africa loyal to the Crown – by trying to placate the Nationalists on the colour question – that the politicians ultimately lost the very link that they were trying to maintain.

And anyway the majority of Afrikaners were never really won over to the cause of Crown and Commonwealth. The republican ideal never died. On the other hand, with the establishment of a republic a certain duality in the minds of some English-speaking South Africans – that tug of war between identifying oneself with England or South Africa – fell away. Once the link with the Crown had been broken, they were obliged to think only in terms of their own country.

To the majority of South Africa's population – the Africans, the Coloured people and the Indians – the switch to a republic made very little difference. Changes, for better or for worse, could come under either regime.

And the Crown itself? Had its efforts, through among other things the visits of various members of the royal family, done anything towards keeping alive this connection? Had these royal ambassadors achieved any success? Not in practical terms and not in the final analysis. But then, these visits were never expected to achieve much more than the engendering of a feeling of goodwill. And this they certainly did. The bright-eyed Prince Alfred, the conscientious Prince George and the dignified Princess May, the debonair Prince of Wales, the hard-working King George VI with his radiant Queen and his unspoilt daughters – all these, and others, did what they could to strengthen the tie between the Crown and the country. Yet their efforts seemed hardly more than thistledown in the winds that blew so strongly in Southern Africa.

But one thing they did achieve. To a country beset by so many problems, they brought, from time to time and for brief spells, an all-transcending aura of romance. In all the pomp and the glamour and the colour and the excitement of these royal visits, one experienced at least an illusion of unity. To watch the extraordinary enthusiasm of all the country's people – black, brown and white – was almost to believe that all hearts beat as one. As these royal ambassadors passed, they spread an exhilarating, unifying, indefinable magic, such as no politician could ever do. That magic has been lacking ever since.

BIBLIOGRAPHY

BOOKS

Adcock, St J.: *The Prince of Wales' African Book.* Hodder & Stoughton, London, 1925.

Alice, Princess, Countess of Athlone: *For My Grandchildren,* Evans, London, 1966.

Anon: *The Visit of H.R.H. Prince Alfred to the Colony of Natal.* Jarrold, London, 1860.

Battiscombe, Georgina: *Queen Alexandra.* Constable, London, 1969.

Bisset, Major-General: *Sport and War.* John Murray, London, 1875.

Bolitho, Hector: *Edward VIII.* Eyre & Spottiswoode, London, 1937.

Bolitho, Hector: *George VI.* Eyre & Spottiswoode, London, 1937.

Collins, W. W.: *Free Statia.* C. Struik, Cape Town, 1965.

Dalton, John N. (editor): *The Cruise of H.M.S. Bacchante 1879–1882* (2 vols). Macmillan, London, 1886.

Deakin, Ralph: *Southward Ho!* Methuen, London, 1925.

de Kock, W. J., and D. W. Krüger (editors): *Dictionary of South African Biography*. Tafelberg, Cape Town, 1968–72.

Donaldson, Frances: *Edward VIII*. Weidenfeld & Nicolson, London, 1974.

Epton, Nina: *Victoria and Her Daughters*. Weidenfeld & Nicolson, London, 1971.

Field, William Osgood: *Things I Shouldn't Tell*. Eveleigh Nash & Grayson, London, 1924.

Gore, John: *King George V: A Personal Memoir*. John Murray, London, 1941.

Hancock, W. K.: *Smuts* (2 vols). Cambridge University Press, Cambridge, 1968.

Hattersley, Alan F.: *The Natalians*. Shuter & Shooter, Pietermaritzburg, 1940.

Inglis, Brian: Abdication. Hodder & Stoughton, London, 1966.

Innes, Sir James Rose: *Selected Correspondence 1884–1902*. Van Riebeeck Society, Cape Town, 1972.

Juta, Marjorie: *Boundless Privilege*. Human & Rousseau, Cape Town, 1974.

Krüger, D. W.: *The Age of the Generals*. Dagbreek, Johannesburg, 1958.

Legge, Edward: *Our Prince*. Eveleigh Nash & Grayson, London, 1921.

Longford, Elizabeth: *Victoria R.I.* Weidenfeld & Nicolson, London, 1964.

Magnus, Philip: *King Edward the Seventh*. John Murray, London, 1964.

Mallet, Marie: *Life with Queen Victoria*. John Murray, London, 1968.

Marie Louise, Princess: *My Memories of Six Reigns*. Evans, London, 1956.

Marquard, Leo: *The Story of South Africa*. Faber & Faber, London, 1955.

Martin, Theodore: *The Life of H.R.H. The Prince Consort* (5 vols). Smith Elder, London, 1877–80.

Middlemas, Keith: *The Life and Times of George VI*. Weidenfeld & Nicolson, London, 1974.

Morrah, Dermot: *The Royal Family in Africa*. Hutchinson, London, 1947.

Nicolson, Harold: *King George the Fifth*. Constable, London, 1952.

Paton, Alan: *Hofmeyr*. Oxford University Press, Cape Town, 1964.

Perridge, Major Frank: *The History of Prince Alfred's Guard 1856–1938*. E. H. Walton, Port Elizabeth, 1939.

Pope-Hennessy, James: *Queen Mary 1867–1953*. George Allen & Unwin, London, 1959.

Potgieter, D. J. (editor-in-chief): *Standard Encyclopedia of Southern Africa*. Nasionale Boekhandel, Cape Town and London, 1970.

Price, G. Ward: *Through South Africa with the Prince*. Gill, London, 1926.

Redgrave, J. J.: *Port Elizabeth in Bygone Days*. Cape Town, 1947.

Roberts, Brian: 'Prince Affie: How they came to Durban', *Daily News,* Durban, 13 April, 1963.

Robinson, A. M. Lewin: 'The Portrait of Prince Alfred by Frederick R. Say', *Quarterly Bulletin of the South African Library*, March 1973.

Rutherford, J.: *Sir George Grey*. Cassell, London, 1961.

Sencourt, Robert: *The Reign of Edward VIII*. Gibbs & Phillips, London, 1962.

Smuts, J. C: *Jan Christian Smuts*. Cassell, London, 1952.

Solomon, Saul: *The Progress of H.R.H. Prince Alfred Ernest Albert through the Cape Colony, British Kaffraria, the Orange Free State and Port Natal in the Year 1860*. Saul Solomon, Cape Town, 1861.

Stow, George W.: *Thoughts on Britain and Her Destiny: A Poem dedicated by permission to H.R.H. Prince Alfred on the anniversary of his birthday, 6 August, 1860*. Smith Elder, London, 1861.

van der Byl, Piet: *The Shadows Lengthen*. Howard Timmins, Cape Town, 1973.

Varley, D. H.: 'Bowler, Baines and the Breakwater', *Quarterly Bulletin of the South African Library*, March/April 1952.

Verney, F. E.: *H.R.H*. Hodder & Stoughton, London, n.d.

Victoria, Queen: *The Letters of Queen Victoria 1833–1901*. John Murray, London, 1908–32.

Walker, E. A.: *A History of South Africa*. Longmans, London, 1957.

Wallace, Sir Donald Mackenzie: *The Web of Empire*. Macmillan, London, 1902.

Warner, Constance: *History of the Kimberley Club*. Kimberley, 1965.

Wheeler-Bennet, John W.: *King George VI*. Macmillan, London, 1958.

Wilson, G. H.: *Gone down the Years*. George Allen & Unwin, London, 1947.

Wilson, Monica, and Leonard Thompson (editors): *The Oxford History of South Africa* (2 vols). Clarendon Press, Oxford, 1971.

Windsor, The Duke of: *A King's Story*. Cassell, London, 1951.

BROCHURES AND MAGAZINES

Illustrated Souvenir of the Visit of T.R.H. The Duke and Duchess of Cornwall and York. 1901.

His Royal Highness. Issued by the *Natal Witness* to commemorate the visit of H.R.H. The Prince of Wales to South Africa, 1925.

The Grahamstown Training College Magazine, September 1925.

With the Prince in the Cape Peninsula, April 30 – May 4, 1925.

The Prince of Wales's Visit to Johannesburg, 22–25 June, 1925.

JOURNALS AND NEWSPAPERS

The Graphic, The Illustrated London News, The Owl, South Africa, The Sphere.

Die Burger, Cape Chronicle, Cape Argus, Cape Times, Diamond Fields Advertiser, Diamond News, Eastern Province Herald, Natal Daily News, Natal Mercantile Advertiser, Natal Mercury, Pretoria News, Rand Daily Mail, The Star, The Times, Die Transvaler.

NOTES

PRINCE ALFRED

(1) Queen Victoria ('very *short . . .*') – Victoria, *Letters.* Victoria ('in his middie's . . .') and Albert on Alfred – Martin, *Prince Consort.* Victoria ('should have as few ...') – Victoria, *Letters.* Alfred ('full of fun and life ...') – Martin, *Prince Consort.* Alfred ('darling Mathilda . . .') – Field, *Things I Shouldn't Tell.* Albert ('What a cheering . . .') – Martin, *Prince Consort.* Immobility etc. of British royalty – *The Times.* Albert ('in the development . . .') – Martin, *Prince Consort.* Victoria and King Leopold – Victoria, *Letters.*

(2) 'A truly royal progress' – *Argus.* All other quotations in this section from
Cape Chronicle.

(5) Stow's poem – Stow, *Thoughts.* 'Boisterous weather' – Solomon, *Progress.* Ball ('spacious ...') – Redgrave, *Port Elizabeth.*

(6) Grey ('Nothing ...') – Martin, *Prince Consort.* Alfred and *faux pas* – Bisset, *Sport and War.* Grahamstown ('which prides . . .'), tribesmen ('They charged . . .') and Sandile ('They were in ...') – Solomon, *Progress.*

(7) Dirty Boys' Corps – Collins, *Free Statia*. Hunt ('that glorious day ...') —Bisset, *Sport and War;* ('doubtful whether a hunt . . .' and 'yelling Kaffirs') – Collins, *Free Statia*. ('Most of the sportsmen . . .') – Bisset, *Sport and War*. Alfred's reception ('great enthusiasm . . .') and Grey's speech — Collins, *Free Statia*.

(8) Affie in Natal ('Through the back door . . .') – Roberts, *Prince Affie*. Alfred ('the general expression ...') – Anon, *The Visit of H.R.H.* Cheering – Roberts, *Prince Affie*. Railway ('Away we went ...') – Solomon, *Progress,* and ('Whatever festivities . . .') – Roberts, *Prince Affie*. Cowell to Prince Consort – Martin, *Prince Consort*.

(9) 'At first our hearts . . .' – Solomon, *Progress.* Victoria on Alfred – Victoria, *Letters*.

(10) 'Even those who took part . . .' and 'He has always said . . .' – *Diamond News.* 'We are part and parcel . . .' – *Cape Chronicle.* Grey ('carries away . . .') – Martin, *Prince Consort.* Coloured woman ('He is *my*. . .') – Solomon, *Progress.*

(11) Alfred's death ('intemperance') – Mallet, *Life with Queen Victoria.*

PRINCE EDDY AND PRINCE GEORGE

(1) Dalton and the Queen ('Prince Albert Victor . . .' and 'a great fear . . .') – Nicolson, *George V.*

(2) Prince George's diary ('We are going . . .') – Nicolson, *George V.* Queen to Alexandra ('The *Bacchante* ...') – Victoria, *Letters.*

(3) Princes ('We admired . . .') – Dalton, *Cruise of H.M.S. Bacchante*. Eddy ('I think the eldest . . .'), and Georgie ('your impudent snout ...') – Nicolson, *George V*. Princes ('We have kept as quiet . . .' and 'driving there by Rondebosch . . .') – Dalton, *Cruise*. Georgie ('we passed an ostridge . . .') – Nicolson, *George V*. Princes and Cetshwayo – Dalton, *Cruise*. Georgie ('16 & 17 stone . . .') – Nicolson, *George V*.
(4) Georgie to mother ('This is really...') – Nicolson, *George V*. Malay deputation – Dalton, *Cruise*. Eddy ('the Queen has no more loyal . . .') – *Cape Argus*. Eddy ('the sad circumstances...' and 'Cape Town . . .') – *Cape Times*. Dalton on South African situation – Dalton, *Cruise*.
(5) Princes ('At 4 a.m. . . .') – Dalton, *Cruise*.
(6) Queen on May ('very sensible . . .') – Pope-Hennessy, *Queen Mary*.

PRINCE GEORGE AND PRINCESS MAY

(1) Princess May (*Ophir* and 'Her Royal Highness . . .') – Pope-Hennessy, *Queen Mary*. May ('slight unapproachability . . .') – *South Africa*.
(2) Prince George on Kitchener – Nicolson, *George V*. Zulu spokesman ('the sun had set . . .') – *South Africa*.
(3) George to Edward VII ('He wished me . . .'), Monarchy's thanks ('the loyalty and . . .') and Chamberlain's opinion ('have a very good . . .') – Nicolson, *George V*. George ('Never in our history . . .') – *South Africa*.

THEO ARONSON

(4) Arrival in Cape Town ('a *lovely* morning . . .' and 'It was all so simple . . .') – Innes, *Correspondence*. Prince George's speech ('Apart from . . .') and architecture ('Fundamentally . . .') – *South Africa*. George to Alexandra – Pope-Hennessy, *Queen Mary*. James Rose Innes ('I was kept bobbing ...') – Innes, *Correspondence*. George on May ('Darling May . . .') and George to May ('Somehow I can't tell you ...') – Pope-Hennessy, *Queen Mary*.

PRINCESS CHRISTIAN
(1) Victoria on Helena ('I consider the matter . . .') – Epton, *Victoria and Her Daughters*. Victoria on Christie – Mallet, *Life with Queen Victoria*. Grave-robbers ('sweepings of the streets . . .') – *South Africa*. Alexandra on 'The Snipe' – Pope-Hennessy, *Queen Mary*. Princess's visit ('Though the journey . . .' and 'The sinking of political . . .') – *South Africa*.
(3) Gift of diamonds – *Diamond Fields Advertiser*. King George VI ('a little family...') – Marie Louise, *My Memories*. Visit to Rhodesia ('would give Rhodesians . . .') – *South Africa*.
(4) Princess's comment on grave – *South Africa*. Marie Louise and Smuts – Marie Louise, *My Memories*.

THE PRINCE OF WALES
(1) All Duke of Windsor's quotations in this section – Duke of Windsor, A *King's Story*.
(2) H. G. Wells – Legge, *Our Prince*.

(3) Party on *Repulse* – Verney, *H.R.H.* Princess Alice to Queen Mary – Princess Alice, *For My Grandchildren.* All other quotations – Verney, *H.R.H.*

(4) Prince's speech ('the happiest . . .') and Afrikaans ('Gentlemen . . .') – Ad-cock, *African Book.* Princess Alice to Queen Mary – Princess Alice, *For My Grandchildren.* Speech – *Cape Argus.*

(5) Unless otherwise indicated, all quotations are from Verney, *H.R.H.* George V on dancing – Pope-Hennessy, *Queen Mary.* Prince on tours – Windsor, *King's Story.* Pretoria Choral Society – Adcock, *African Book.* Prince on Johannesburg – Windsor, *King's Story.*

(6) Unless otherwise indicated, all quotations are from Verney, *H.R.H.* Slogan – Marquard, *Story of South Africa.* Prince and Solomon – *South Africa.*

(7) Prince and girls ('But on the other hand . . .') – Verney, *H.R.H.* Prince and African girl – Wilson, *Gone down the Years.* Cecile Smith – *Grahamstown Training College Magazine.*

(8) Prince and polo and 'a damp and . . .' – Verney, *H.R.H.* Marjorie Juta ('By Jove . . .' and 'We returned') – Juta, *Boundless Privilege.*

(9) Prince on Smuts, and on Boydell – Windsor, *King's Story.*

(10) Leader writers – *South Africa.* Nationalist member to Prince ('Prince, we want you . . .') – Verney, *H.R.H.* Minister to Prince – Windsor, *King's Story.*

(11) Prince's education ('on the trade routes . . .') and King-in-Waiting – Windsor, *King's Story.* Journalist ('What is excusable . . .') – Sencourt, *Edward VIII.*

THEO ARONSON

Hertzog's opinion on marriage – Donaldson, *Edward VIII*.

THE ROYAL FAMILY
(1) Table Mountain ('clean-cut . . .') – Morrah, *Royal Family*. Queen at Banquet ('As the Queen . . .') and Smuts ('You must do this . . .') – Van der Byl, *Shadows*. Coloured ball – Morrah, *Royal Family*.
(2) Smuts on royalty ('This is just . . .') – Hancock, *Smuts*. Smuts on tour ('our South African people . . .') – Morrah, *Royal Family*. Queen to Queen Mary – Wheeler-Bennet, *George VI*. King and Afrikaans – Van der Byl, *Shadows*.
(3) Queen's magnetism – Van der Byl, *Shadows*.
(4) Queen's conversation ('I am so glad . . .') – Van der Byl, *Shadows*.
(5) Singing at Lovedale – Morrah, *Royal Family*. King William's Town ('By *command* . . .') and King in Transkei – Van der Byl, *Shadows*.
(6) Incident on entering Free State ('Why was I . . .') – Van der Byl, *Shadows*. Monarchy and Bloemfontein ('The thoughts . . .') – Morrah, *Royal Family*. Queen on South African crowds – Van der Byl, *Shadows*.
(7) Family group ('Come and look . . .') – Van der Byl, *Shadows*. Story about rugby player ('I saw your Mom . . .') – private information. King and mayoral chain – Van der Byl, *Shadows*.
(8) Luthuli's speech – Morrah, *Royal Family*. Queen on Zulu dancing – Van der Byl, *Shadows*.

(9) Work of royalty ('It is one long grind . . .') – Van der Byl, *Shadows*.

(10) Africans in Rhodesia ('more closely . . .') and Governor's reception ('leading members . . .') – Morrah, *Royal Family*.

(11) Margaret ('And what about Mummy's?') – Warner, *Kimberley Club*.

(12) Elizabeth's dedication speech – Morrah, *Royal Family*.

(13) General Kemp – Smuts, *Smuts*. Queen on President's widow – Wheeler-Bennet, *George VI*. Malan on meeting – *Cape Times*.

(14) Smuts and Table Mountain – Smuts, *Smuts*. Smuts and Hofmeyrs and Smuts on Queen – Paton, *Hofmeyr*. Speeches at luncheon by Smuts and King – Morrah, *Royal Family*.

(15) Smuts on royal visit ('Never . . .') – Morrah, *Royal Family*.

10388868R00137

Printed in Great Britain
by Amazon.co.uk, Ltd.,
Marston Gate.